MY MESSY BEDROOM

My Messy Bedroom

Love and sex in the 90s

Josey Vogels

Véhicule Press

Cover art direction and design: J. W. Stewart
Cover photograph: Thomas Leon Königsthal Jr.
Cover border illustration: Marie Lessard
Cover imaging: Beattie & Martin
Interior design and imaging: Simon Garamond
Printing: Imprimerie d'Edition Marquis Ltée

CANADIAN CATALOGUING IN PUBLICATION DATA

Vogels, Josey
My messy bedroom : love and sex in the 90s

Collection of weekly columns from Hour magazine.
ISBN 1-55065-064-5

1. Sex. 2. Love. 3. Man-woman relationships.
I. Title

HQ16.V64 1995 306.7 C95-900280-4

Published by Véhicule Press, P.O.B. 125, Place du Parc Station, Montréal, Québec, Canada H2W 2M9
Distributed in Canada by General Distribution Services.
Distributed in the U.S. by Inland Book Company, New Haven, CT

Printed in Canada on acid-free paper.

To my Dad, who I know would have loved to be have been here for this

Thanks to:

My Mom, a pillar of strength who, despite her impeccable housekeeping, was always tolerant of my messy bedroom.
My slew of brothers and sisters whom I love with all my heart and soul and to whom, I know, I will always be "drolakapuff"
Audrey my teacher and sexiest friend in the world
Wanda and Linda for knowing me all my life and still liking me
Li for hours of long-distance phone therapy, wisdom, and love. I couldn't do it without you
Jillian for the enthusiasm, love, and the spinach kugel
Nancy & Sarah for all the bagels and laughs around your kitchen table
Ilana, I miss you
Laurel, still part of me
Dan, you must be getting a real kick out of all this
Chuck, super editor, advisor, extremely tolerant male subject, and dear friend
Colin, hey buddy you're great
Martin, Jamie, and Peter, and Tracy for listening to me whine and complain and be a bitch every week at work

All the folks at *Hour* for supporting my habits
David, a total sweetheart of a guy, who helped
whenever I asked, let me be a stress queen and bought me
dinner when he couldn't keep up with
all the attention I demanded
Thom for giving me great cleavage and
Marie and John for being so talented

And the rest of ya, you know who you are.
You drank beers with me, inspired me, and constantly
told me how wonderful I am, and we know how
much I love that.

Contents

Going All the Way

Sex for Sale

Me and the Girls

Welcome to My Messy Bedroom

THE ONLY COMMON GROUND we all share when it comes to talking about love and sex in the 90s, is that we can't shut up about it. Of course, while sex has become appropriate dinner-party discussion, some of us still have trouble talking about it in our own bedrooms.

Beyond that, both love and sex–and yes, the two are mutually exclusive–are pretty much open to interpretation.

Thanks to feminism, the "free love" of the 60s, Hollywood, therapy, self-help and how-to books, radical primitivism, and a renewed conservatism, we are now blessed with sex in the 90s: a nice mix of openness, repression, confusion, pierced body parts, and Guess jean ads.

These days, we have feminists producing porn alongside born-again virgins. We're experiencing the dawn of virtual sex, attending S&M trade shows, and shopping at sex supermarkets.

In the meantime we're still trying to meet "the right guy"

and obsessing over the wrong ones. We complain about our insensitive men while we moan about our inner thighs. We want pleasure but we're still nervous asking for it. We want commitment as long as it's not too demanding. We want control except when we don't.

Sex may get confusing but at least it's never boring. Well, maybe sometimes. That's when we dig out the manual. But beyond "the joy of sex," our obsession with it goes beyond just feeling good. Sex gets us excited about a lot of things. For women, sex is about power and learning how to enjoy ourselves while holding in our stomachs. As for men, we're led to believe the most important thing is penis size. Well? They're starting to talk.

So whether it's a matter of taking things in your own hands and feeling good about it, exploring the fine art of cruising, getting dumped, enjoying your fantasies, pornography, or *Cosmopolitan* magazine, it's all scattered throughout My Messy Bedroom. It's where contradiction sits on the dresser right there with the tube of lipstick and the jar of cellulite cream. Where the mess piles up until that last pair of stretched out underwear riding up my butt tells me it's time to deal with the dirty laundry. And, it's where I have had some of the best and worst sex of my life. Come on in. I'll tell you all about it.

Lookin' for Love

I Love You

I LOVE YOU.

Probably the most overused and, at the same time, difficult-to-master phrase in our vocabulary.

It certainly isn't like they write it in Hallmark cards, or love songs, or trashy romance novels. I mean, how much love is brooding in your heart when you have to come up with some generic and appropriately clichéd verse that is to be coupled with some tacky pastel floral image, reproduced a million times, and sold for a coupla bucks a shot?

One can love football or Fettucine Alfredo without hesitation. Loving people is where it gets messy. Especially the ones you have sex with. That kind of love isn't something we're taught to understand. Beyond the idea that we're supposed to fall into it and live happily ever after.

Why do you think it means nothing in tennis? Okay, I'm a cynic. But when it comes to love, who isn't? That's because learning to love in a healthy, fulfilling, physically and emotionally satisfying way is the most brutal and exciting challenge we face. That's why we're in such desperate search of it. The problem is, just like shopping for that perfect gift for a dear friend, you can never find exactly what you're looking for.

"Excuse me, do you have anything in a nice shade of…sensitivity, strength, and good looks, with a solid sense of humour?"

Of course, you can always find something that might do in the meantime. The selection is varied and endless in this department. Lust, crushes, infatuation, and casual sex will always tide you over. Obsession is another nice option. You get the intensity, even the irrationality, you'll find in the early stages of falling in love. And with obsession, these feelings usually last way longer. But how are you supposed know when it's really it?

As far as I know, no one has ever done a scientific study of what percentage of your daily thoughts must be taken over by someone to indicate that you are, in fact, in love. As in, "I have stared out this window, avoiding my work, thinking about him for exactly 45 minutes now." Does that qualify as love?

Or, if I'm doing the dishes and my mind wanders to the thought of his mouth eating the things that were once on the now-crusty, half-empty plate of pasta that we left because the wine that accompanied the meal took over and suddenly our naked bodies were entangled on the kitchen floor, are we in love?

Or, how does that old saying go... (okay maybe it's not so old, but it is fast becoming so, at least among my friends), you know you're in love when you can fart in front of him.

As you have probably surmised, I'm no expert.

One thing's for sure; we love love. And that's partly why we end up so confused by it. Marketing departments the world over have exploited our infatuation with the concept. It has all the hooks: seduction, drama, intrigue, and mystery. Of course, we all know how misleading advertising can be. It's never as pretty as it looks on the box. Not that this stops us from spending enormous time and energy shopping.

Then, despite all our efforts, we go running scared when the real thing is staring us down. Sure, most of us can make it last through the initial you-can-do-no-wrong and the thinking-about-you-makes-me-feel-all-warm-and-squishy stages. Sometimes you even get as far as the maybe-it's-not-absolutely-necessary-to see-you-nine-days-a-week-28-hours-a-day stage. But then you face the inevitable: the expiry date, only it's never marked on the damn package. It just creeps up one day. You're sitting on the couch and all of sudden.... his forehead looks weird.

That's my specialty; finding the one fault that means it just won't work. Like, you're totally head-over-heels, but he's a bad dresser. You get fixated and can't stop thinking about it. It's a downward spiral from there. Next, you realize the earth-shattering sex you thought you were having is actually boring and predictable. Your head is filled with doubt and you come up with some lame line to get out of it as quickly as possible.

"Umm....I'm real sorry, but I'm busy for the rest of my life ..." Anything to save you from those blood-sucking monsters, Intimacy and Commitment.

You don't wanna mess with those guys. You might have to actually work at it.

But lust and passion are so much easier to come by, you say. Maybe you like spending your life falling madly in love, having your head twisted around for a few months, getting dumped, and then spending months twisting your head back straight again. Maybe it's self-affirming for you to twist someone else's head around for a few months, then dump him, boosting your self-esteem when he comes crawling to you, snivelling for you to take him back.

How can spending hours negotiating the power dynamics of your relationship, compromising your differences, and carrying someone's baggage once in a while, compare to that?

An Obsession

ADMITTING YOU HAVE A PROBLEM is the first step.

Unfortunately, unlike alcohol or drug addiction, obsession is often harder to kick.

One person I talked to was obsessed with someone for six years. My own worst case lasted a good year. (Though, like alcohol or drugs, some would say you never really get over it. You think you can handle that one social drink, but bam, even a taste sets you off again.)

No one wants to become hopelessly obsessed with someone they can't have, or wouldn't necessarily want if they could have them. It's one of those inexplicable things that happens, like losing socks at the laundromat.

No one *chooses* to sit at home waiting for the telephone to ring or to check their answering machine 300 times a day, just in case. When you're obsessed, you have no control over your behaviour. You *have* to act like a complete idiot.

When you're obsessed, aliens temporarily possess you and make you do things like comb all the bars frequented by the object of your lust, "just looking for a friend."

They cause you to get really drunk every time you do see him (obsession is very thirsty work) and inevitably end up blathering about how cool you are with the whole thing. "I just want to sleep with you, really."

He, succumbing to the ego stroke, decides to believe it and goes home with you. And you, watching him dress immediately upon awakening, end up hating yourself, knowing you've just broken every rule in the girl book.

But then obsessions go against all the girl book rules anyway.

No way are you supposed to walk 13 miles out of your way to "coincidentally" run into a guy on his way to work.

Calling drunk or "just dropping by" his house at 3 a.m. is also less than empowering. Mind you, real pros do their best to avoid this. Mastering the art of obsession means salvaging the maximum amount of pride possible. For this, it's best if you have experience on both sides, then you know what doesn't work. Having been an obsessee at some point in your life is the key to learning the tricks of being a successful obsessor. Cardinal rule: do not do unto others what you would not want them to do unto you.

During the denial stage, this, of course, means you'll be

doing a lot of wallowing, either alone or amongst friends. Of course, once your friends are sick of hearing about your misery, you mostly end up alone sitting in your apartment listening to Barry White songs for hours on end, replaying those three dates you had and investigating possible meanings for every word he uttered. "I wonder if when he said he wanted to work things out with his ex-girlfriend, he meant he wanted to dump her and be with me?"

When your contributions to conversations are all prefaced with, "That's just like (insert whatever code name you have assigned obsessee)," it should become clear that you need help. But while it quickly becomes painfully obvious to everyone around you that you're in severe need of the twelve-step program, we all know that "you have to want to quit."

More likely you'll instead enter into the rationalization stage. While all your friends have fully concluded the guy's a jerk and can't understand what such a great person like you sees in him, you make excuses for him. And besides, what's wrong with a little obsession, the masochist in us says, it's better than nothing, right? It's true that obsession can sometimes be a good stop-gap measure (nothing like a bit of heartache and rejection to make you feel alive). It just takes some of us a little longer to realize that the energy would be much better spent on getting a life.

Besides, you can hone lots of wonderful life skills throughout an obsession. You can tap into your theatrical talents when he's around by mastering the art of acting cool, clever, and popular as hell, convincing everyone that you've never been better in your whole life when, really, your stomach is nestled comfortably in your throat and you feel like you want to throw up. You get to pretend you're not actually waiting for the phone to ring, trying to sound as nonchalant as possible when it actually does and it's actually him. "Oh, have you been trying to call? Because I was out doing loads of wonderful fun things... how ya doin'?"

You can practice your conversational skills by spending way too much time coming up with all the clever things you'd say if you actually did "casually" run into him the seventeenth time you walk into the same bar.

Being obsessed can also expand your musical taste because, when you're not wallowing in Barry White, you're listening to the tape he made you or the band you've found out is his favourite. Same goes for films.

You make new friends because you want to meet everyone who knows him even remotely to pump them for information, and you end up at parties you might never go to because you know he might show up.

Then it happens: it's 7 a.m. at one of these parties and you've just spent the last two hours talking to the last guest, a complete loser of course, keeping one eye constantly on the door, in case he shows up. It is at this point that it should dawn on you that something is awry, that maybe you need a new hobby.

That his "I wish it could be different" you have steadfastly believed to be a sign that there's a chance, isn't.

That if you could just have that one more chance to talk to him, you would feel better. You won't.

That feeling that there will never be anyone else like him. There will.

It's time to make a clean break.

Getting over obsession is tough. And yes, it leaves scars. Time is really the only cure. Mind you, that six-year one I mentioned ended most ironically (or satisfyingly, depending on your taste for revenge). The guy finally came around, and she quickly discovered she wasn't interested. 'Nuff said.

Leggo My Ego

IT EVEN TURNED UP on "Beverly Hills 90210." A true sign of the topic's cultural relevance.

"Men and women aren't necessarily monogamous by nature; Eskimos even have a word to describe the close bond they all feel in sharing the same lover." Remember that unfortunate "feminist" character they had for a while—the independent and opinionated, sex-crazed, manipulative, divorcée anthropology prof? This is what she told Kelly in her "Women and Anthropology" class: "Traditional monogamy only works when everyone adheres to the same morality."

Of which, of course, this woman has none because she's just gone after Kelly's boyfriend Dylan.

"Relationships can be healthier if people are more honest about their sexual impulses," nympho-anthro prof concludes.

After wrestling with that one a bit, our darling Kelly

reveals, "I guess I'm just an old-fashioned girl."

Social order is restored. Monogamy rules.

I don't know if monogamy is natural but I do know there are as many takes on the concept as there are cultures in the world.

Most of us are raised with the idea that if you make a commitment to someone, naturally, you don't sleep around. It's that simple, right?

Yes, according to a friend of mine who volunteered his approach. When he starts seeing someone he lays it on the line right up front. "You're free to see anyone you want," he tells the interested party. "But if you start seeing someone else, you won't see me anymore."

Sounds more like blackmail, I told him.

"Hey, everything has a price," was his blunt response. "Sometimes you just gotta make choices."

I'm not so sure.

The word itself sounds like some kind of virus.

Oddly enough, *Webster's Dictionary* defines monogamy as "the condition" or "the habit" of having only one mate.

As if it was some kind of addiction.

I think a friend of mine is hooked. She was trumpeting her virtuosity the other day. "I never cheat on the people I go out with," she stated proudly.

This person goes out with a new person practically every

week. "But I never cheat on them," she insisted.

Serial monogamy.

There are some fuzzy lines when it comes to monogamy. For instance, how far do you have to go to constitute having cheated on someone? Holding hands? Kissing? With tongue or without?

Is there a cheating free zone? That is, if you're in another city or another country and you fool around on someone, does it count?

Then there's the "I can sleep with other people but you can't" approach. Uni-monogamists. They're always amusing.

On the other hand, the concept of an "open relationship" has always made me suspicious. These inevitably become a battle of the egos. "Hmmm...you stomped all over my ego last week when you slept with that person, so this week it's my turn to destroy yours, okay?"

"Sure, I'm cool about it."

Yeah, right.

That's the problem with monogamy. It gets mixed up with our egos.

If your partner sleeps with someone else, you rant and rave that he or she has violated every trust, destroyed everything you have built together, but the bottom line is that the idea of your partner being physically intimate with another person makes you want to vomit. How could you choose him over me? What's wrong with me? Was she better than me?

Sometimes fooling around is just about sex, not love. The two *can* be mutually exclusive, at least that's what the person doing the fooling around thinks.

People often tell me that if you're in a relationship, and you feel the need to sleep with someone else, there's something wrong with the relationship. I don't know if I buy it. I don't believe people have affairs simply because they're having relationship trouble. One poll I read said that almost half of the men and women they questioned in monogamous relationships cheat. The reasons: 96 percent of the men and 74 percent of the women said "feeling horny" was enough of a reason. Reason number two was that the other person was "just so gorgeous." Deep.

I have to admit, the idea of sleeping with the same person for the rest of my life is a bit scary. It's gotta get boring after awhile. And no matter how many *Cosmo* articles you read about how to "put some spice back into your relationship," maybe you just need to sleep with someone different, fresh, new. I'm not saying that you necessarily should. Obviously, acting on the impulse creates some problems, but denying it exists at all can sometimes create more.

My friends in long-term "monogamous" relationships

assure me you can work this stuff out. One of these long-distance friends says she copes by living all her promiscuous fantasies through her single friends. I spend a lot of time on the phone with her.

Monogamous by nature? I have my doubts. It seems like more of a practical choice given our social structure, conditioning, and collective morality.

And our egos.

Wanna fight?

IT ALL STARTED WITH A PAIR OF PANTS. I thought they were fabulous. From the 60s, never been worn, straight-legged, mustard with deep-green pinstripes. A real score at $8. Quality time between us had been at a premium and I was tapped, having spent the bulk of my time on the bare necessities: work and sleep. Getting bare was confined to the shower between the latter and getting ready for the former. We were both frustrated and a little out of touch.

In my world, scoring cool, cheap clothes is like a religion. It automatically follows, then, that scoring something for your date is the ultimate declaration of love, right? What better way to show how much I really cared. So the day after finding the pants, full of excitement and anticipation, I presented my polyester peace offering to my guy.

He hated them. He actually laughed when I showed them to him. I was crushed. I figured we might as well break up right then and there. What was the point? We were obviously worlds apart and he simply didn't understand me at all. He certainly couldn't love me. I burst into tears.

He tried them on in an attempt to comfort me. I thought they looked fantastic. He still hated them. ("I'm a strictly-denim kind of guy," he says, that honesty I love so much, punching me in the gut; his flair for always having "good jeans" suddenly meaningless.) I felt worse. I got angry. How could he be so mean, so unappreciative, ungrateful, and stubborn? And so lacking in taste? How could he not see what I saw, appreciate things the way I did?

Before we knew what hit us, the few yards of material had unravelled into everything that was wrong in our relationship. Our emotions soared and it wasn't long before neither of us had a clue as to what we were actually fighting about. All I knew was that I was right. Of course, we handled it like adults. He stormed out, frustrated, perplexed, and pantless, leaving me sitting on my couch, alone in my apartment, sobbing.

That's the great thing about a good fight. It can make the little things in life seem so important. Forget about world poverty and famine, I just wanna know why you never want to go out with my friends?

Yes, most of these fights only pretend to be about something really important. The "petty" fight is usually pretty easy to get to the bottom of. All it takes is for one of you to calmly initiate a reality check and do a little digging. Stress, sexual frustration, your menstrual state, or too much coffee will usually turn up as the culprit.

But the way fights get played out can be most revealing. Some might even admit that knowing how to fight well with your partner is even more important than good sex. And like sex, it's easy to get into a rut. The subject may change, but the routine doesn't and pretty soon you start to feel like you're having the same fight over and over.

I'm the nag. I never let anything go. The slightest shift in mood, change in expression, nuance in vibe doesn't escape me. He's standing half an inch farther from me than usual. I start. "What's wrong?" "Nothing." "C'mon, what's wrong?" "Just forget it." "C'mon, talk to me." "I don't want to talk about it." "Fine." Silence. That's when I really kick in. "I have ways of making you talk," I glare.

Then I get accused of picking a fight which starts another fight. This is good. As long as you keep the conflict intense you can avoid dealing with what's really going on. Senseless screaming and irrational statements take so much less thought. Since we're better at this, he will soon fall silent and start staring blankly at the TV, clicking like a fiend.

Take a breather, then go for the kill. Provocation strategies are rather personal. Use whatever works for you.

Of course, that doesn't mean you have to like what he

says when you do finally manage to drag something out of him. Especially if he's the kind who reacts to provocation by going on the defensive. Between his defence and your offence, you might as well forget any grasp on reason and head right into if-you-say-another-word-my-head-is-going-to-explode frustration. Usually followed by a little more silent treatment.

This is the final test. At this point, if you can both walk away, calmly, (that means no running after him out the door in your underwear) and regroup, you may stand a chance. You can both cool off and deal with whatever was there in the first place—if it really was anything—later. Of course this requires patience and letting go of your masochistic bloodthirst for conflict and that nasty evil monster with the power of 100 men, insecurity.

And the reward is you get to make up. Which can sometimes take care of the sex thing too. Fighting can be wicked foreplay.

Commit Me

FRIENDS GET A LOT OF LEG ROOM. If they don't get around to calling for a while, that's okay. A friend can be a blubbering mess one day, together and full of wisdom and insight the next. Up, down, weak, strong, however my friends are feeling, I can usually work with it and manage to enjoy a long, fulfilling relationship with them.

Why not lovers? Have sex with someone and suddenly you have to tuck away all your weaknesses, self-doubt, and that bottle of mustache bleach you keep in the bathroom. Basically anything even slightly resembling a too-human quality or fault. One slip-up and you're toast.

Hey, I might not be perfect, but that doesn't mean I can't demand it in my date, right? When the object of my desire eventually starts revealing himself for the hideously human creature he is, why should I be expected to put up with it? I'll just hold out a little longer until that perfect someone comes along, or hell freezes over, whichever comes first.

For my parents—who grew up together, dated as teenagers, married, and stuck it out for 44 years—commitment was a given.

These days, commitment is like a disease and, if you believe *Cosmo* (who doesn't), it's somewhat of an epidemic. "What Scares Men Silly About Commitment," "How to Spot a Commitmentphobe," "Men, What Makes Them Commit." They're always on about it.

Meanwhile, of course, us women have it all figured out. Sure, I can commit to a relationship, save for that little bit of side action I like to hang onto.

What stops us from taking the plunge? I'm not talking commitment as in 'til-death-do-we-part and can-you-pick-up-my-shirts-at-the-cleaners commitment. Just the kind that allows you both to switch off the radar, sit back, relax, and enjoy yourself without looking over your shoulder all the time. (Yes, I realize that's the only way you'll see Mr. Right if he suddenly walks into the room.) Without getting bored.

Of course, it may be true that the right one simply hasn't come along yet, but—just to get it out of the way now so it doesn't suddenly dawn on you when you're all alone, chowing down on the strained pears at Shady Rest—the following signs could indicate that you are suffering from what is known to the *Cosmo* girl as a "fear of commitment."

■ At parties, you introduce your date as your cousin, just in case.
■ The 10 per cent you don't like about him completely overshadows the 90 per cent you love.
■ "I have a lot of stuff to work out" is the most common phrase in your vocabulary.
■ You never do anything about all that stuff you have to work out.
■ The thought of waking up at 65 with this person make your palms sweaty.
■ You've been going out for more than a year but still can't plan anything more than a few hours in advance.
■ When she wants to talk to you about the relationship, you suddenly have "a bunch of stuff to do."
■ There is always a "but..." lingering at the end of that little "I love you" phrase.
■ Your mouth suddenly develops a nervous twitch when you try to use the word "we."
■ When you go to restaurants, you can only decide what to order by eliminating everything else on the menu.
■ Your grade-school teacher was always on your case about "shaaay-ring."
■ You're forever wondering if there just might be something better out there.
■ You go away on vacation and "forget" to tell him.

■For you, the terms "comfortable" and "familiar" don't belong on the same list as relationship.
■You love the chase.
■You're under 35.
■The kitchen tap isn't the only thing that is hot and cold when you're around.
■Sex is about pleasure–yours.

Even the best relationship is not all smooth sailing, but there's no sense even trying in a leaky boat.

A couple words of advice for those who find themselves in a commitmentally-challenged relationship.

Get out!

Yeah, I know you want to wait it out because you know he'll eventually see the light and come around. Two more words: He won't. Not before he's had his way with your self-esteem, patience, and faith in humankind. Or you're chokin' down those strained pears.

Scary Stuff

MAYBE SOME OF US just aren't cut out for relationships. I mean, who said we could all be good at it? Some of us excel in other areas, right? What's the big appeal of something that is statistically guaranteed to run out of passion in something like 1.349 years anyway?

And what's so wrong with being alone? I get all the companionship I need from my friends. They understand me and they're not nearly as inconsistent, draining, or frustrating. So why do we bother? I think it might be because no one has been able to determine what's more painful: being in a relationship or wanting one.

It'd be a whole lot easier if it weren't for that glorious part at the beginning. I fall for it every time; sucks me right in. The good stuff, the charged, edge-of-your-seat stuff.

Then things always start to give. All that lust seems to turn to labour just when we become less interested in working at it. Why is it that we work our butts off getting someone to like us but as soon as we're in a relationship with them, we're ready to throw in the towel after the first coupl'a rounds.

1) **Fear.** The biggy. Some would say sheer terror is at the root of 95 percent of all relationship problems. If you're scared, you'll find any excuse for why it won't work. "My relationships never work because I get out of them before anything real happens," says one friend, who once broke up with a guy because he made too much noise with his knife and fork when he ate.

Fear can make you jealous, possessive, defensive, and yes, utensil-usage-sensitive. It can turn simple insecurities into a minefield and a poor self-image into a punching bag. Fear laughs at any sense of independence and relishes in neglect. "It's your problem not mine" is its favourite line; projection its most effective tactic. Vulnerability and fear have a great relationship. Fear stops you from trying. If you don't try, you can't fail, and you won't make yourself vulnerable.

2) **Lack of communication.** After fear, this is the next biggy and my personal favourite (as in, "If only he would communicate..."). While it's closely tied to fear (opening up to another person is, well, terrifying), communication deserves some individual attention. In the early do-no-wrong stages, your mate's reflections on the price of fruit

may make for gripping dialogue, but eventually, the novelty wears off and you have to start revealing the truth about all those things you made up about yourself so the person would like you. Better to clam up than reveal that you actually *weren't* raised by wolves.

Of course, the flip side to this is an incessant need for communication. Motivated by a fear (see what I mean about the scary factor) of the unknown, ("What and why are you holding back?"), sometimes you just have to realize you can't get blood from a stone. Thumb screws and stretch racks only cause pain if someone really has no information. If you're lucky, he'll make stuff up, but you'll probably just end up giving the relationship a spinal injury. 'Cause once you get on this roll, it's never enough. Could this constant testing of your date's ability to spill his guts maybe stem from some unrealistic...

3) **Expectations.** While perfection is a lofty goal, it quite simply doesn't exist. Besides, it's boring. (What would you do after?) Face it, you're never gonna find someone as perfect as you. If you find you're constantly in relationships that don't meet your standards, it could be one of the those excuses for not doing the work.

Of course, if you know you won't be happy unless you're with someone who at least shares a remote interest in doing something with his life and you're going out with a deadbeat, you could probably stand to live up to your expectations a little more. Which brings us to...

4) **Differences.** As in different expectations, different backgrounds, different values, different ideas of romance, marriage, family, different tastes in music, different levels of education, success, and being at different stages in your lives.

Differences like these may seem unimportant, even charming, when you first set out, but they often take on a life of their own. They have been known to single-handedly destroy a relationship. Differences can only be conquered with sheer determination. Of course, if you have very different attitudes about how much difference a relationship can take, you may be out of luck. Truth be told, sometimes your differences are just, well... too different. It simply may be time for...

5) **Change.** This subject usually makes its first appearance in a relationship in the form of, "You're going to have to change (your ability to communicate, your expectations, the way you handle our differences, your smelly socks more regularly, etc...). Once you realize you've milked the person of all their change potential (takes about a minute if you're really sharp) and changes are not up to your satisfaction, change may simply mean, "Things have changed."

"Why do you get a haircut?" was the insight offered by a

fellow relationship-challenged friend. "Sometimes you simply need a change." And sometimes, we just have to admit we make...

6) **Bad choices**. "Why don't my relationships work?" asks RC-friend #2. "Because I choose to go out with idiots, who have no desire to have motivation, or are self-centred assholes." (None of these are mutually exclusive, of course, and all are undoubtedly connected to, yes once again, reason #1 and may be insurmountable because of reason #2.)

In some cases, the relationship never should have been a relationship at all. (Like a one-night stand that just got a little carried away and all of sudden you realize it's turned into a 20-year marriage). Suffering a bad relationship can sometimes seem easier than admitting that you made a bad choice, getting out of it, and starting all over again.

Scary stuff.

A Family Affair

I COME FROM A LARGE FAMILY. As the last of eight kids, my existence is, begrudgingly, the one thing I have to thank the Roman Catholic Church for. If it hadn't been for my parents' firm belief in their faith's concepts about family planning, they probably wouldn't have got to me.

But even my dad eventually realized how ridiculous it was to take someone else's word for what was best for him and my mom when it came to family. As a poor, immigrant farmer, struggling to make a way for himself, eight kids was not exactly the key to career advancement. As for my mother, well, spending six out of 13 years pregnant, pretty much nipped a career outside the home in the bud.

The notion of family is an odd one. Who didn't, at some point in their growing up, wonder about the fairness of being obligated to this group of people you felt nothing in common with just because they were your family? In my life, I have often felt much closer to the network of friends

I have created around me than to my own family unit. I mean, I love my blood ties, but sometimes it just strikes me as odd that we're supposed to accept and try to get along with our family just because we're born into it.

People keep desperately clinging to the notion that if we tamper with this institution, the world will end and we'll all be stuck with unused family season passes to Disney World.

As far as I can see, most of the people around me spend much of their adult life trying to undo all the damage their good traditional family values have done to them. Having a "traditional" family guarantees neither good nor value.

I suppose traditional family values do create employment. What would Oprah et al do without being able to probe the damage they cause? Family therapists, group homes, shelters, a whole industry would crumble without traditional family values to keep them in business.

While the demise of the nuclear family and the subsequent feared fallout is often credited to everything from feminism to vegetarianism to rock'n'roll music, the accusers never question the concept. Maybe it just doesn't work. At least, not in the narrow vision we still get shoved down our throats.

Religion and morality have always been used to justify traditional notions of the family. Suburbia was created to accommodate the nuclear family invasion. Even TV has tried to keep us on track: from the days of domestic bliss with "Father Knows Best" and the Cleaver clan through to when things started to get rough for the old institution. Then shows like "Family Affair," "The Brady Bunch," and "The Partridge Family" tried to reflect different images of the family. Eventually we found out Florence Henderson took a particular liking to her eldest stepson and David Cassidy became a drug addict.

Goes to show you, you never really know what goes on behind the scenes. And the more we try to hide behind some idealized tradition, the more it will backfire.

Remember those corsets they used to make women wear that looked great from the outside but cut off our circulation, crushed our insides, and made us faint? Well, we've learned to live without them. In fact, we found we could breathe a whole lot easier once they were gone.

Women now wear styles that fit our needs; some of us go for the conventional, some for what's comfortable. We're still tugged at by social norms, but at least the options are greater.

I think we need family. But we need to broaden the definition. It doesn't work the way they first thought it would. Time to go back to the drawing board.

I like one person's suggestion that we open up the concept completely. Choose your own family. Remember fantasizing as a child about adopting someone else's family? People close to us, not necessarily our sexual partners, a network of people around us who support and love us. Why should you have to get "married" or have a regular sex partner for a set period of time to get all those cool benefits?

Getting Dumped

THE LAST TIME SOMEONE DUMPED ME, I pined for almost a year. At least my ego pined for almost a year. While I was sure at the time that he just couldn't see how perfect we were for each other, once I got over it, my sense of reality resurfaced and my ego emerged from the rubble and returned to its former fragile state. In other words, I finally convinced myself he was a jerk.

The best dumping stories always happen in high school though, before you learn to at least try to muster up enough ego and pride to force you to act calmly and rationally. Stealing the keys to my boyfriend's mother's car and taking off in that beautiful red Chrysler Magnum after he told me it was over, is one I still hold dear to my heart. That was when I could still appreciate a good dramatic scene.

Now that I'm all grown up of course, I handle break-ups with cool maturity and reason. Yeah right. After I dump a beer over his head.

The ideal way to avoid being dumped is to dump him before he has a chance dump you. Even more gratifying, if you can pull it off, is to see the signs, then strategically turn things around so that he changes his mind, decides he does want to be with you, then you dump him.

Of course, both of these require recognizing the signs of an imminent dump. These range from the gag-inducing obvious: lines like "I love you but I'm not in love with you," "I think we should start seeing other people," "Maybe you love me too much," or "I just want to be friends." (Just a note to the dumper. Any of these lines is akin to saying, "Can I have your heart so that I can crush it under my heel and then run it through the laundry with my dirty underwear." Skip it. At least have the guts to be honest.)

Then there are the more subtle signs. Like the person shows up for a date with another woman.

If, for some reason, you happen to miss the signs (at this point, I suggest you avoid crossing streets where oncoming traffic might be an issue), you're heading for the big dumping station. It's located down loser lane, right next to the depths of despair department.

Now, as I mentioned, even though you want to take the person's eyes out with a fork, if they actually have the guts to come out and say, "I think we should stop seeing each other," you must, and I repeat, must, for that moment, pull yourself together (you'll have months of opportunity to fall apart), be cool, maybe even throw in an "I understand," and walk away.

Okay, I will take this moment to admit that it's not easy for the dumper either, having to be so cruel and all.

That out of the way, back to the victim. It's a bit of haul, this getting dumped thing. Of course, you could take the fast-food route to recovery and simply jump in bed with the first person who shows interest and start the cycle all over again. This is known as the "I-can't-be-alone syndrome" and can last several years of your adult life. Like any other pattern, the longer you maintain it, the harder it is to break. No, if you want real recovery, you have to suffer. The following is a handy guide to the stages following a good dump and the measures you can take to experience genuine relief.

Stage #1: Wanting to get even

This is a volatile stage. Be careful. Enjoy your anger while it lasts. Just don't act on it. Remember high school? Instead, chant "scumsucking pig" quietly throughout the day and fantasize about what you *would* do to him if you *were* still in high school.

Stage #2: Denial and release

Better known as the "bury it in beer" stage. Go out and party your brains out if you must. Just stay away from the real hard stuff and listen to your body when it's screaming surrender. We're after release, not total annihilation.

Stage #3: I-can't-go-on detox

This is when it hits full force and you must cry at all times. In the shower, in the subway, in line at the supermarket. You must also spend a lot of time in bed crying and listening to hurtin' music.

Stage #4: Relapse

After detox, you may find yourself wanting a fix. If you simply must call him, don't. When you break down and finally do call him, don't try to convince him to get together. When you do convince him to get together, don't sleep with him, at least not more than once or twice. But don't beg… too much.

Stage #5: Help, I'm alone!

Once humiliation and feeling completely pathetic and sorry for yourself has run its course, a general state of panic sets in. This is followed by the realization that you actually have to *do* this being-alone thing. This stage involves some humiliation because you have to call up those girlfriends you've been ignoring because you've been so enjoying being treated like shit. Also included in this stage is a world that suddenly seems to have been taken over by nauseatingly happy couples everywhere you go, along with constant reminders of him. Fun, fun, fun.

During this time you will receive many solicited and usually many more unsolicited words of comfort and advice. Between the sensitive "Get a life" and the cliché "There's lots more fish in the sea," a few gems will hopefully slip in, and may even make their way into your brain, like: "You deserve better." Okay, it's cliché, but self-affirming. You need all you can get at this point. It's the only way to get to....

Stage #6: Rediscovery of self

This stage is usually signified by a drastic haircut or a fabulous new outfit. Anything that makes you look absolutely irresistible will do. A good test to see if you're really here is to then "turn up" looking fabulous wherever your dumper might be hanging out. Walk by, flip a casual hello and smile over your shoulder. Don't be too cool, however, they'll know it's an act, and they'll get to feel smug instead of you, cause they'll know you still care.

True, this is only fun when you've still got some pent-up hurt and anger, but be sure you're genuinely on your way to recovery or you may experience total relapse. Especially if you show up and he's with someone new. Be warned! That sudden urge to run him over with a truck is only your ego getting revved. Don't let it convince you to do foolish things, like grab the first man who walks by and thrust your tongue down his throat.

If you get through this last stage, recovery is within reach.

And, if you're really mature, you may even want to begin attempts to become friends with the person, that is, if there really was something you liked about him or her in the first place.

We're All in This Alone

On Your Own

BEING SINGLE IS GREAT! If it's summer and being single means freedom and frolic. Inevitably, however, summer reveals itself for the mating season it is and we are left in the cold reality of winter. If you don't manage to find someone to bed down with, you've got some serious sloggin' ahead. Winter, as we know, is when social contact screeches to a halt. The streets become as barren as our souls. We get pasty, hideous, grumpy, and sexless and are left diddling our way through the TV-filled months ahead.

A few tips:

■ Renew all your XXX-video club memberships.

■ Update your literature: *Playgirl* is out (mind you, it was never in, unless you're gay, of course), *Future Sex* is in.

■ Pool your resources with single girlfriends for bulk purchase discounts on batteries.

■ Get "on-line" with all the other losers. Post e-mail to the alt.not.getting.any. newsgroup.

■Forget clothing swaps, get together for fantasy swaps. Trade in some of those tired old fantasies for some more appropriate to the season—"take me naked in a parka" or "let me lick your galoshes."
■Develop a phone network among single friends. That way you can bond on who's lonelier and provide each other with constant reminders of how shitty that last relationship was and, really, how good it is for you to be alone. (Be sure to keep a schedule of who you call and how often, in order to keep ears relatively fresh.)
■Decide you don't need anybody else to be happy.
■Come to your senses.
■Come on to the 16-year-old who works at the corner store for kicks, just to check if you've still got it.
■Read a lot of pop psychology about why you can't seem to have a relationship. Blame: father/mother/society/self (the latter, of course, only as a last resort.)
■Waste a lot of time coming up with "if only I was" reasons for why you can't seem to have a relationship. (Smarter, prettier, thinner, richer—any will do, really.)
■Rent *White Palace* (or your own favourite sex-scene film) for the seventeenth time and fantasize about James Spader (or your own favourite sex-scene participant).
■Eat. (Be sure to stock up on chocolate.)
■Get drunk. (This is where the phone network comes in

handy. Be sure to consult schedule.)
■Eat some more.
■Sleep a lot. (In fact, eat a lot and think about sex right before you go to sleep and hope for erotic dreams.)
■Watch a lot of bad TV. Fantasize about Jake/Billy on "Melrose Place," Dylan/Brandon on "Bevery Hills 90210."
■Eat some more.
■Go to the gym.
■On second thought, resolve to go to the gym.
■Make some other resolutions you won't keep, like never to call up that old boyfriend you couldn't stand but had great sex with, even if you're desperate.
■Call ex-boyfriend, see if you can convince him to have sex with you.
■Practice Kegel exercises to get you in shape for next summer.
■Join the Alliance for Chastity and become a born-again virgin.
■Take up needlepoint.

Most importantly, remember, summer's just around the corner. In the meantime, happy diddling.

Loving Yourself

IT USED TO BE SO GREAT. When we first discovered each other I was young and full of curiosity. I'd spend hours exploring, seeking out new sensations, new ways to please. I'd let my imagination take over, fantasizing about all the crazy and exciting things I'd like done to me. I used to take risks, fondly fondling under restaurant tables, in dark movie theatres or other places where the risk of being discovered was half the excitement.

We've been together for years now and I'm afraid things have become mechanical. The passion is gone. I get off, roll over, and go to sleep. Wham, bam, thank you, ma'am.

I don't know when things changed. I mean, this is the last person I need to hold back or be shy with. I know every nook and cranny of her body, I've learned to accept, even love her faults, her quirks, her moods. She is the one I am most comfortable with and least intimidated by. According to the experts, we should be having mind-blowing sex. So why does it sometimes feel as automatic as doing the dishes?

I started talking to other people to see what they did, how they kept things exciting. "I like to dress up in different outfits," one woman told me. Someone else told me she likes to talk dirty, another said she fancies a little restraint, usually of the leather persuasion.

So what happened to me? Those long leisurely mornings in bed, getting myself in the mood, teasing, playing, touching, where did they go? I was becoming my own worst lay, a real disappointment in the sack. No foreplay, just straight to the main event, over almost before I could get to the juicy bits of the dirty story in the dog-eared magazine held strategically in my free hand so my fingers could turn the pages without losing the rhythm. Maybe I just didn't love myself anymore. How could I possibly love anybody else?

It was time to take things into my own hands and feel good about it. I needed to stop succumbing to the myths of a society that simply could not accept such hedonistic selfish sexual pleasure. "Playing with yourself" because it was fun, not because I wasn't "getting any" elsewhere: *Masturbation: Sex Life of a Loser*, coming soon to a dark, seedy porn cinema near you, starring yours truly. Forget it!

Damned it if I was going to let my innocence, curiosity, and zeal be once again usurped by the guilt that had been so carefully cultivated in my youth. I was smarter than that.

Surely I had overcome the belief that deriving pleasure from touching myself "down there" really was sinful and would land me an afterlife sentence "down there," hadn't I? My eyesight was fine and my palms hairless after all.

So why did I still feel so guilty? Why did I still view sex with myself as anti-social and self-indulgent? Was it that it really *was* just a replacement, a substitute for "the real thing."

Enough's enough. I'm making a plea for guilt-free self-love. I say let wanking take its rightful place in the continuum of recognized sexual activities!

Truth be told, sometimes sex alone is actually better than some of the "real" sex I've had. And when you're not getting any, it's no substitute, it's *it*. And besides, wanking is good for you. It releases stress, helps you sleep, and gets you in touch with your body. It's also a much more fun way to procrastinate than cleaning your apartment and—added bonus—it's safe.

Most studies reveal that about 60 percent of men and 40 percent of women masturbate. (Toss in all those who are still too embarrassed to admit it and guaranteed we're talking closer to 80 or 90.) And most of these statistics show that among those who pull their pud, half feel guilty afterward.

What is that? Really now? Reams have been written on how to improve your sex life with your partner. But what about the one we truly love, the one who is always there for you, the one you almost always still respect in the morning? The possibilities are just as endless and privacy, trust, and communication (the most difficult barriers to good sex with a lover) are usually already worked out.

Maybe I need to spend more quality time with myself; flirt, drive myself wild whispering sweet nothings in my ear. Or get kinky, tie myself up, buy some sexy lingerie, dress up for myself, even go all out and treat myself to a pulsating shower head.

Once jacking off (or "jilling off," as we girls like to say) takes its rightful place as part of a healthy approach to sexual pleasure, we can pass it along to future generations. No longer will young girls be left in the dark for years, oblivious to their capacity for pleasure, feeling cheated because of so many pleasurable formative years lost just because no one ever let us in on the secret. Instead of ending up feeling resentful because boys learn about their "thing" from the moment they first pee standing up and we don't clue in until our first boy-bike experience, we can teach both boys and girls to be proud of their capacity to please themselves, and raise them with the tools and techniques we all need to truly love ourselves.

Nice Butt!

HOW COULD HE HAVE KNOWN her breasts were hormone packs? Her pouty lips and sexy Latin accent made no reference to what lay below. The way she teased, "I lika ya mawth," was charming. "And she was soooo cute," my friend told me of the seductive stranger he met while on vacation in San Francisco.

Of course he'd love to go back to her place. He was pumped. But the "one little thing" she thought she better reveal to him before she actually revealed *it* to him proved to be the glitch in what was otherwise a perfect specimen of my buddy's "ideal" babe. She was a he.

Ah, but looks can be deceiving, can't they?

What attracts any one person to another is probably right up there with the Caramilk secret as one of life's great mysteries.

It's also the most subjective question in the world. What attracts one person repulses another. It could be their smell, the way they carry themselves, their earlobes.

Unlike cats and dogs, we can't go around sniffing each other's butts to see if we fancy someone. We've developed much more civilized ways of determining our attraction to another person: Mmmm... Nice butt!

Yes, like most complex and completely incomprehensible questions, we have no problem coming up with simple, generalized statements about what gets our mojo workin'.

"Eyes." "Eyes." "Eyes." "Eyes, but hands come in a close second." "Eyes." This unofficial survey would make it seem that the days of butt- and leg-men are gone. Could it be a sign of men's developing sensitivity that is making them opt for safer body parts?

"They're lying," countered one of the many women I asked who cited sense of humour (we're so deep) as what turned her crank. "And a developed upper body, of course."

Another respondent pointed out that both eyes and sense of humour are ridiculous answers. "What am I gonna say? 'Man look at that woman across the street, great eyes, and what a funny hat, she must have a great sense of humour.'" *He* starts with the face and works his way down.

As evidence of the question's fickle and circumstantial nature, one respondent simply answered: "I'm too desperate right now to answer that question."

No, despite all our standards and model requirements,

little can explain that moment when your eyes meet, you share a sly smile, and Bingo! a voice inside you screams: "Get over here and do me, now!"

Of course, little escapes science, and the lab coats think they've got some answers. When it comes to attraction, it seems we're not completely unlike our sniffing, four-legged friends. Apparently, something called pheromones in our sweat may have something to do with what makes you suddenly feel like jumping in the sack with the person you're standing next to in the hot, smoky bar you're in.

Within moments, the theory goes, pheromones trigger I-wanna-do-you hormones which travel at warp speed through your loins and, depending on how drunk you are, to your head, where they match up with the checklist you have compiled from a lifetime of programming. Information from as far back as your childhood about values, what you want and need, and what you find desirable all come to play in what or who makes you squirm.

Perhaps my childhood practice of hiding under the couch with all those dust-bunnies waiting for my brothers and sisters to come home from school so I could jump out and surprise them explains my tendency toward the rumpled, dustmop look by which I am so enchanted.

Anyway, those in the know believe this "blueprint" also goes towards explaining why the majority of us are attracted to people of similar backgrounds, cultures, and classes. Some researchers have even documented cases where people chose a partner whose name began with the same letter. "That's Gerry with a 'G'? Shucks, sorry."

Research also reveals that we never end up with our ideal types. This gives us something to fall back on when things don't work out. (I had to end it. He was too perfect for me.) Or it just underlines how unexplainable attraction is.

In fact, a crazy thing like attraction seems a rather reckless method to rely on in finding a mate. I put more thought into buying a new coat I fancy than plunging headfirst into a relationship with the guy I fancy. I guess that's why it's so exciting.

Or frustrating. Probably the most common complaint when it comes to attraction is pheromonal imbalance. This is evident when the person you are attracted to is wildly attracted to your pheromone-oozing best friend, sitting right next to you.

Cruise Control

"At the beginning of the night I separate them into the 'Yes baby, you're the one' category right through to 'Absolutely no way.' Of course, these categories shift as the evening progresses. By last call, you just want someone to agree you're there."

—*Ye Olde Book of Bar-stool Philosophy* by B. A. Slut.

AMERICAN BIOLOGIST Timothy Perper has spent thousands of hours in bars, both gay and straight, researching the fine craft of cruising. In biology lingo, he calls it the "mating ritual" (kinda lends it a legitimacy, don't you think?). His description is almost poetic, referring to it as a dance, with well-choreographed, calculated moves. You leer at me, I leer back. You move in on me, I continue flirting or I tell you to get a life. Pure art.

As is fashionable these days, Perper started his research by comparing our pathetic behaviour with that of animals. Have you ever seen a dog work the park? But Perper doesn't necessarily buy today's other fashionable argument that we do this out of duty, as some instinctual way of maintaining our species. (Great excuse, though, huh? "I have to go slutting, the human race is counting on me.") For one, Perper points out, if reproduction was the main concern, how does one explain the heavy cruising that goes on in gay bars? No, Perper figures, with us modern folk so uprooted and scattered about, we're simply desperately seeking some kind of human interaction, some contact. In other words, never mind the futile search for this intangible thing we call romantic love, people just wanna get laid.

Now, having spent thousands of hours in bars participating in the mating ritual, I have to say, most of the behaviour I've seen out there would probably leave most animals scratching their heads and heading back to the jungle, where it's safe.

For one thing, they don't serve alcohol in the jungle. Booze fuels the human mating ritual. Picking people up stone cold sober is definitely not in our nature.

And animals can't talk, so they can't engage in bad pick-up lines or take a sudden interest in appliance repair or whatever uninteresting topic you manage to come up with when you strike up conversation with a total stranger over a pulsating disco beat.

No, meaningful is not what most people are after when they're cruising. "I'm not searching for Prince Charming,

I'm just looking for someone half-decent who's worth dating," was the sentiment offered by one cruisaholic. Fair enough. I mean, what are the chances that "the one" just happens to be the guy who groped you as you squeezed through the crowd on your way to get a drink?

Of course, we all know that actually ending up in a relationship as a result of a bar encounter is a long shot. I think the probability rates are up there with winning the lottery. As the saying goes, "Every relationship that starts in a bar ends in a bar." The most it's usually good for is a little ego boost, some proof that you've still got it, or some insight into what you need to get it. If you're lucky, or, in some cases, simply strategically positioned at the bar, you may land yourself some interactive tongue-diving and, if you're really lucky—the grand prize—some bad sex at the end of the evening.

Tony offered me the results of his own studies on cruising, gathered from three years of research as a bartender in a popular downtown heterosexual meat market. "Because of the environment, you don't have to be extra cautious about what you do. You don't have to be real clever, even be a good flirt." Yes, it's true, bar cruising has its own special language.

Lecherous drunk guy: "So, where you from?"

Me: "Uhhh... Outer Space."

Oblivious Guy: "Oh wow, can I have your phone number?"

Yeah, I see what you mean, Tony.

Consider this: It's 11 p.m., Thursday night, in a renowned pick-up joint downtown. Me and five girlfriends are out "cruise testing." The place is crawling. I've barely checked my coat when some guy has whisked me over to meet his buddies. I'm suddenly expected to converse with some joker in sunglasses who says he's from LA.

Groan. We barely have time to make up stories about who we are when that scene's moved on and we're onto the next. Within seconds, we learn that, as five babes in a place like this, eye contact is at your own risk. At one point, I looked at a guy and the next minute he was practically sitting in my lap. So much for the desire to test my flirtation skills. Obviously, they decided to do away with that stuff. Waste of time. Full body contact is the rule here.

"Yup," confirms Tony, it's pretty much a free-for-all. "A woman walks by and a guy will grab her and say, 'Hey, can I buy you a drink,' and she'll say yes or no. If it's yes, great, off they go, if it's no, he just moves on to the next."

But men aren't the only aggressors, he insists. Women are into the game too. "There's an underlying agreement, and you sign it just by walking into a bar like this."

We finally score a table, slightly away from the main action. Seated, I feel a little more in control. The room is nothing but darting eyes and lurking men. In fact, looking around, given the ratio of men to women, it could easily be mistaken for a gay bar. In some sick need to disprove the theory, my friend and I decide we'll go to the washroom. Sure enough, en route, my brave buddy is practically pinned to the bar by someone wanting to buy her a drink. "Uh, your friend's pretty direct," I remark casually to his buddy. Silly me, what an invitation. I might as well have said "Let's do it on the floor right now." But, as bartender Tony promised, a simple brush-off did the trick. I was ready for the next level. The dance floor!

"When the dance floor starts to fill up, things really start to happen," says Tony.

One of the admiring male onlookers surrounding the display case—I mean, dance floor—voiced his approval: "Wow!" (These guys really had a way with words.) Before I knew it, I was surrounded. Wow-boy was shimmying up and down my body and I had had enough. I was in the wrong market. Way too little supply for the demand.

I suppose we could save ourselves all this grief and just line up everyone in the bar and simply pair them off; it's probably about as meaningful. But then we'd be denying ourselves that wonderful challenge: the thrill of victory, the agony of defeat. And something to do on Saturday night!

Takin' It Easy

I WAS SITTING IN A BAR with a male friend whose over-extended single status was causing him much grief. He had reached the "I'd just like to get laid" stage.

A simple demand, no? "It's so much easier for women," he whined. "You can pick any guy you want." Yeah, just like picking out a nice head of lettuce or your favourite ice-cream flavour, right? Truth is, the one you want only ever appears when you're with a date or having a bad hair day. Then, of course, you have to factor in the probability that he is already attached or gay.

But it's not just timing. Guys get suspicious if it's just sex we're after. First of all, women never *really* just want sex, right? We may be after your package but the package we're really after is follow-up, commitment, or, if applicable, your money. If we really just want sex, we're cock-teases, sluts, used goods, or desperate—so unbecoming. No challenge and bad for the ego.

Mind you, same goes for us. If a guy seems too eager to get it on, it's a big turn-off. "What's wrong with him?" we wonder. Or if that's all he wants, we wonder, "What's wrong with me?"

When you think about it, seeking out casual sex is really anything but. Beyond the obvious considerations in the monogamy-means-never-having-to-say-you're-HIV-positive morals of today's society, there are plenty of very uncasual things about "casual" sex.

Like waking up after a one-night stand. This can often be far from casual, especially if the one-night stand involved alcohol, which it often does in our sexually dysfunctional society. Nothing like a few drinks to loosen up the old hormones, eh? It's amazing how that "Oh, my head... where am I... oh yeah... groooan," feeling can make you suddenly remember a pressing early Sunday morning appointment.

Then there's the post one-night stand. Depending on the success of the original event, you may suddenly be overcome by the urge to tie your shoe or to slip your grocery bag over your head if you see the guy approaching on the street.

There are some positive things about one-night stands. They can be a great pick-me-up between relationships or during dry spells. This is identified by the "one-night stand glow," when you show up for work the next day with a slightly too-wide grin on your face and colour in your cheeks, or hair like Geena Davis' in *Thelma and Louise* after she spent the night in a hotel room with Brad Pitt.

Sometimes, the best approach to casual sex is to avoid the sex part of the equation. This is known as the have-I-still-got-it test. These encounters don't necessarily have to culminate in sex, merely in the undeniable possibility of it. Then you go home alone, get a good night's rest, and achieve the glow without having to deal with all the other crap.

If it's actually sex more than a quick ego boost you're after, casual sex with friends can sometimes work for a while. Being "friends-who-fuck" or having a "fuck buddy" can be a convenient way to get some without having to deal with the risks, rejections, or repulsion of trying to pick someone up in a bar or at a party. Though this kind of casual sex can be like a nice warm glass of milk; soothing, comforting, but it eventually sours. One of you meets someone else or wants to expand the term "friendly."

So much baggage for a single sleepover, it hardly seems worth it. Except that not that all casual sex and one-night stands are about satisfying purely physical needs or boosting egos. There are some one-night stands that you want to turn into a series of one-night stands, then a relationship.

Some even argue that no one *really* wants casual sex, that it's merely a convenient term to describe that awkward undefinable period before either party feels secure enough to call it a relationship. Or to call it off.

I guess that's how you end up with casualties.

Going All the Way

And the Survey Says...

WHAT'S BECOME MORE POPULAR THAN HAVING SEX?

a) talking about it.

b) writing about it.

c) responding to questions about it.

Yes, welcome to sex in the 90s in North America, where the poll has replaced men's poles as the focus of our sexual attention. Every week someone new is asking us whether we're getting it, how often we're getting it, whether we're doing it on our backs, up the bum, tied to the ceiling, or with our neighbour's pets.

We may be unable to share our most intimate secrets and desires to achieve satisfaction with our partners, (at least 31 percent of us according to one poll), but we're sure eager to expose ourselves publicly to achieve the big statistic.

Sex in America: The Definitive Survey got more coverage than most penises, if we look at the still relatively low rate of consistent condom use evidenced in these polls. This was the study that came out last year and comforted us with the revelation—as interpreted by every mainstream newspaper and magazine—that we're all having boring, uninspired, monogamous sex. Keeping up with the Joneses only meant keeping it up about once a week, and Mr Jones was usually only keeping it up for Mrs Jones. Whew, pressure's off.

Other, um... I guess, *less* definitive surveys have given insight into international sexual habits, Generation seX, what men want, what women want, what women think men want, and what men think women think that men want. The neighbour's dog is probably one of the few whose sexual habits haven't been charted. Give 'em time. "Excuse me, Fido, do you prefer humping your owner's leg to actual sex with another canine?"

Perhaps this obsession with anonymous, public sex is a way of making up for our statistically lacklustre sex lives. As one commentator put it, "Sex surveys are the closest most of us get to group sex." Or maybe it's a way of exercising our voyeuristic tendencies. "I just wanna peek at what the Joneses are doing." Or perhaps, without all those numbers to compare ourselves to, we would have no way of knowing how wonderfully average we are. "Well, at least

I'm as good/bad or not as bad as the Joneses." Sadly, when it comes to sex, the desire to be normal is often more seductive than desire itself.

Besides upholding the status quo and fuelling the you-too-can-improve-your-pathetic-sex-life industry, what exactly is all this number-crunching worth?

Sex in America was supposedly intended to help us figure out what it is about our behaviour that might contribute to the spread of AIDS. Its conclusion: Heterosexuals are pretty much not at risk of getting AIDS because there's so little action between infected and uninfected groups. Now that's a new one and oh, so helpful. "Hey boys and girls, forget the condoms, it's safe now!"

The big problem with all of this inquisitiveness, of course, is that honesty and sex go together like Vaseline and latex. We lie about it, brag about it, or, at best, are seriously deluded. Check it out:

In one survey, 31 percent of men who live with a woman said their partner usually or always performs oral sex on them while only 15 percent of the women said they always or usually do the deed. Hmm... someone's fibbin'.

In another survey, 94 percent said they had been faithful in their relationship while 50 to 75 percent said they had cheated. How odd.

And, if we're all so happily sitting on our picket fences

being ever so faithful and satisfied in our marriages, why is it that half of them end up in divorce? The bliss must be overwhelming.

Basically, if you look at the general results of most sex surveys, not much has changed since Alfred Kinsey started taking notes. Men are still getting the better deal; they have more orgasms than women, masturbate more, think about sex more, get more oral sex, have more casual sex, buy more dirty books, videos, have more affairs...

But stats have a hard time adapting to real life. As a smut-snaffling wanker who adores a good tongue-lashing, I can attest to that. And sometimes all these numbers get taken way too seriously. "Gee dear, I'd love to have sex with you, but we've already done it 1.4 times this week, well above average. Especially since I thought about it at least three times today. Do you think I need help?"

No, in my personal experience, sex surveys are most practical and fun when used to conduct your own private bedroom poll. Having a hard time getting your partner to communicate about sex? Survey them. It's the 90s way to spill your guts. And, by asking your partner the questions directly, you can press for details, and you can usually tell if they're making it up.

The First Time

BEING FROM THE COUNTRY and all, the first time I had sex was an embarrassing cliché. It was in the barn, in the hay. I was 14. He was 16. It was horrible.

"It hurts," I complained, hay riding up my butt. (Haystacks are only romantic in the movies.)

"Just relax," he said, oh so sensitively, as he forged ahead.

I can't even remember if we used a condom. I do remember going to the bathroom later and gathering a small bale of hay out of my underwear. Later, sitting on the couch watching TV with my boyfriend's dad, I was certain he could tell what we had done. I felt like shit.

I've actually demoted the whole thing as my first time on the grounds that I don't believe it really qualified as sex and instead have chosen my second time as my real introduction. It was ideal. I was in a "relationship." I waited before going all the way with him, because he was older and had a bit of a reputation for not being shy about his intentions. (Okay, I was warned to wear steel pants on my first date with him.) I wanted him to prove he loved me first. Two months seemed adequate. The event was practically written for an after-school special. A friend's parents were away, and he lent us their house. My boyfriend brought a box of condoms and we spent the first while playing with them. Blowing them up like balloons and stuff. When we finally got down to it, he took it real slow. If I said it hurt, he stopped. This boy probably saved my sexual life. We went out for five years.

Most of the people I know lost their virginity to the sound of Nazareth blasting in the background so no one would hear. Drunk at a party or in the back seat of a car were the going scenarios.

Like most everyone's first time, my friend's experience has stayed with him. He had a girlfriend at the time, but she wouldn't "put out," so he found someone who would. They did it in the back of her Gremlin.

Guns 'n' Roses would probably be the musical accompaniment today, and I don't think they make Gremlins anymore, but the scenarios probably haven't changed much.

I realize no one can to get anything exactly right the first time. (The guy in the Gremlin didn't come because he couldn't get over the idea that he was actually doing it.) But a little prep would help. Despite all the information about

AIDS, disease, and pregnancy, my 17-year-old niece says few boys will use condoms and the pill is still the preferred method of contraception, usually acquired after you've started having sex. That's probably because the one thing that is still sorely lacking in the education young people receive about sex is adequate training in the art of negotiation.

"A lot of boys won't like you if you ask them to wear a condom," my niece tells me. So a lot of girls don't bother asking. Pregnancy or disease is less immediately devastating than rejection. And you usually can't count on the boy to bring it up. He's got so much on his mind, he usually just wants to get it in as quick as possible before he's too embarrassed to keep it up.

My niece lives in the country, like I did. Despite growing up with sex education in the schools, and increased awareness, sounds like things haven't changed much from Gremlins and Nazareth.Having gone to a strict Catholic school, my sex education consisted of, "You'll get pregnant if you kiss a boy." Of course, they neglected to mention the steps in between.)

The problem with a lot of sex education (when it's allowed at all) is that we are so determined to protect kids from health risks or pregnancy we take the fun out of sex. Kids need to know the risks for sure, but we shouldn't scare them out of enjoying it. Healthy attitudes about sex would be much easier to instill if we would just accept that young people have sex and gave them some practical information on how to do it and how to give others pleasure, safely. Don't all parents want their kids to be the best at whatever they do?

Obviously first times are first times, they're awkward and new and only practice makes perfect. They say languages are easily learned in our youth. If we did some better sex coaching in the formative years, think of all the hours of instruction we could save each other later, as adults.

Lip Service

MMMMM... KISSING IS THE BEST. Remember when you were 12 or 13 and you could suck face for hours? Once you become an adult, you don't "neck" anymore. All of a sudden, it's called foreplay. Which means it eventually involves a decision about whether it'll get around to "sex" or not.

Which pisses me off. Cause you know what happens. You're blissfully lost in all that lip action and suddenly a hand is buried in your crotch. Then you lose it. Consciousness storms in and busts up the party. Lips and libidos are suddenly out of step and your brain taps you on the shoulder and says, "Can I cut in?" followed by "Should I grab his thing now?," "How bloated is my stomach?," and "Am I wearing good underwear?" Any trace of those totally hot kisses you were completely caught up in a moment ago vanishes and next thing you know, your kisser kicks into cruise control and you're en route to that final destination.

No, when it comes to kissing, the best thing to do is to

put sex out of your mind completely. It's not like that option won't be around later if you're interested. In the meantime, take advantage of the sheer pleasure of savouring your partner's saliva and lingering over their lips.

But of course, like a handshake, the way you kiss leaves a lasting impression and says worlds about whatever else you have to offer. So pucker up on the art of smooching.

DO

Linger. What does it take to get a guy to linger? They never seem to worry about wearing out other parts from overuse. Hang out for a while.

Brush your lips lightly across eyebrows, lids, necks, and earlobes, or any other readily or even not-so-readily available body parts.

Tease. 'Til it hurts.

Open your mouth. Close-lipped kisses bite.

Nibble.

Shave. Ever snuggle up to sandpaper?

Practice good dental hygiene. Picking food particles out of each other's teeth is like junk shopping. It's fun at the time but you never know what to do with the stuff afterwards.

Communicate. Say it with saliva, more passionate than words. The perfect opportunity for verbally-challenged men.

Listen. For signals from your partner. If they're panting

heavily or their body suddenly goes limp, there's a good chance you're doing something right. (Though you should probably check if they're still breathing.)

Breathe.

Try to avoid excessive and embarrassing sound effects.

Shift pace and pressure often.

Play. This is supposed to be fun, remember.

DON'T

Insert your tongue unless it's got a purpose. Having somebody else's big wet tongue just lying around into your mouth is right up there with raw-liver sucking.

Deep-tongue dive. Especially suddenly. You may induce vomiting and it won't be pretty.

Slobber.

Belch.

Employ the "If it works, stick with it" approach. It's that too-much-of-a-good-thing thing. Six hours of ear-nibbling is probably a tad excessive.

Check your watch.

Kiss too hard. You don't want to leave bruises.

Kiss too soft. No one likes limp handshakes either.

Suck on your partner's tongue too hard. It hurts, and most of us are fond of our taste buds.

Wear lipstick. It only works in the movies.

Give hickeys. We're only trying to simulate high school here, not relive it.

Talkin' Dirty

TALKING DURING SEX is a bit like talking about sex in public. Some people are comfortable with it, others are not. Some engage in it for the purpose of communicating physical needs. Some people are downright chatty in bed, while others rely on the power of a grunt or a well-toned hmmm.... Some get off on talking, the raunchier the better. Still others prefer things silent, allowing them to enjoy sex as a pure physical sensation... or they're just big-time shy.

Obviously our verbal skills in bed are also determined by our moods, our level of comfort with a person, or with ourselves, how horny we are, or how competent any given lover is.

The approach may vary, but there are some general verbal skills that should always be maintained when it comes to talking during "it."

For example: if you're trying to instruct someone in your

pleasure department, you should try to avoid sounding like a rowing coach. "Now just move that finger/tongue/banana a little to the right, okay a little more pressure... now pick up the speed... and faster...c'mon, keep it up now..."

It's tough. Often, we say nothing, just hoping the other person will figure it out. But, as much as we'd like the power to telekinetically direct others' fingers and tongues, it ain't gonna happen. No matter how skilled a lover is, no two people like exactly the same things, and while some skills are transferable, most have to be adjusted to suit the individual.

Just remember, it's a bit of a minefield when it comes to saying what you want. Proceed with caution. Egos are at stake. Don't say, for example: "That feels about as good as a visit to my gynecologist," unless, of course, you're into speculums and having your cervix examined. Instead, you might want to try something like: "Maybe you could try this for awhile instead, sweetie binkie-poo."

But, the most important thing is you gotta just let go with it. Otherwise you'll lose the moment. You know what I mean. You're lying there, all turned on, enjoying yourself, letting someone else enjoy you. You want to offer suggestions, but you hold off. You're shy or you don't want to say the wrong thing. Meanwhile, your brain is constructing a full seminar and workshop on how to make you come and you end up so distracted by your own self-conscious thoughts that you lose it. You try forcing yourself to relax. HA! Grit your teeth, focus and chant... "I will have an orgasm... I will have an orgasm." At this point you might want to give it a rest and go do your laundry or something.

You don't want to get too analytical when you're talking in bed. No academic dissertations, please. In fact, the fewer words, the better is often a good rule to go by. Let's face it, sex vocabulary is limited. A simple, "yeah... like that" will do. Sometimes, words aren't necessary at all. A few subtle wiggles and shifts can often do the trick.

Sometimes a little more direction is necessary. Hands-on demonstrations can work very well. Besides being a turn-on, watching someone else masturbate can teach you loads. Take notes. A picture is worth a thousand words, as they say.

Another handy trick: Asking the other person what he likes will not only open up possibilities for him, the person might just pick up on it, go wild, and ask you what you like.

Flattery or words of encouragement are good. Just make sure you're honest. You don't want to end up in a situation where you kindly compliment someone for their gentle approach when it bores you to tears. You'll be stuck with it.

A note of caution to men. Never talk about a woman's

body in bed, unless you're worshipping it. And telling someone how much you love her fleshy thighs and belly doesn't count. I'm sure the same goes for men. Discussions of deficiencies are not pillow talk.

Talk itself can be hot. As foreplay, it can really work. Talking "dirty" is a great way to explore fantasies and discover people's limits or desires. It can also really keep things going at a nice clip once you're more involved. And screaming out nasties in the heat of the moment is a great way to introduce yourself to your neighbours .

For the shy one, who'd like to practice his or her verbal skills, a male friend suggested one-night stands as a good time to do some test-runs. He said he talks a lot more with one-nighters 'cause there's less at stake. Mind you, if you're shy, scoring one-night stands might be a bit of a problem.

Talking about sex after sex is somehow easier for a lot of people. Maybe it's got something to do with the 20/20 hindsight principle. We're also less sensitive, more open, relaxed. Same with talking about sex in completely non-sexual situations. It's a great way to pass the time as you're waiting for the bus or in line at the supermarket. It's usually best to be with your partner at the time. Strangers might not be so open to the concept. Then again, there's that one-night stand plan.

Feeling Edgy

I'VE NEVER MET AN ORGASM I didn't like. Sure, maybe I tend to award a little favouritism to the direct, more personal type, but I can usually find it in myself to accept even the most aloof ones, confident that one day they'll cum around.

Yes, from the friendly, outgoing, even boisterous types that march right up and throw themselves at you with vigour and zeal, to the shy, demure types that slink up beside you and catch you by surprise, I enjoy all of their company. They make me laugh, they make me cry, they make me feel relaxed, even guide me to the Lord once in awhile. I know, some are fussy and require extra attention while others are completely elusive, but that's part of their charm. If all orgasms were alike, they'd be boring. It'd be like discovering a new video game. Once you learn all the tricks, the challenge is gone.

But also like a video game, it's often easier to get to the

higher levels playing by yourself. Once a second player enters into the picture, a whole new element of competition is introduced and you become self-consciously aware of your abilities. Why do you think so many women have no problem masturbating to orgasm, but as soon as they're with someone, that simple but glorious pleasure slips away and waits 'til he's gone? The reasons for this are obvious. I'm better at feeding myself and wiping my own bum too.

You know the feeling, girls. You're lying there, he's eagerly savouring the most intimate of delicacies, you've finally relaxed, convinced that today's menu isn't the seafood surprise, and you start getting into it. Soon your body starts twitching, lovely little rushes surge from your toes to your head, and you can feel your face getting flushed.

All of a sudden, the top of his head reminds you that you must dissolve that hair clump in your bathroom drain. Noooo! Not now! you think... focus, girl. You try, you try soooo hard. But it's too late. Your brain takes over. "I'm taking too long. His jaw must be numb. How scrunched up is my face? Do I sound like a bad porn movie? Do I look like a bad porn movie?" At this point, you might as well forget it. (Who says performance anxiety is a male thing?) These demanding, difficult types are best left alone. It's best to let them sulk for a while and set out to discover some other sources of pleasure. Guaranteed that pesky little orgasm will soon be screaming for attention again.

Now I happen to be one of that less-than-minor supposed 40 percent minority of women who requires some sort of direct clitoral stimulation to get off. (By the way, direct does not mean propping up the hood and setting to work. That little protective coating is there for a reason.)

Women's magazines are always telling me to get on top. "It provides more opportunity for manual stimulation," they say. Maybe I'm just not coordinated. And in all the porn mags, couples are always exploding in unison. As far as I'm concerned, simultaneous orgasm is like the rubbing-your-belly-while-patting-your-head thing. Again, maybe I'm a spaz, but I can't do it. To me, orgasms are more like a see-saw. Your partner rides up into the air and you enjoy holding them there, then after a while you exchange thrills. It's still fun for everyone.

Just as my orgasms can range in intensity from a mere flutter to a raging freight train, so can the reasons for my ability or inability to achieve the big oh. If I'm stressed, tired, or drunk, forget it. Sometimes, I'm better off left on my own. Sometimes, I'm better left not getting off.

Still we tend to rely on orgasm as approval—proof that you've had good sex. We want our partner to come, sometimes even more than they do. What can I say? We live in a competitive society, it gives us a sense of achievement.

"Pleasure is more a journey to be savoured than a destination to be reached," I once read. I don't know about you, but I love travelling.

Virgin Again

IT'S OFFICIAL. I am now a card-carrying secondary virgin. Stop laughing, I'm serious. I've decided to re-save myself for marriage. Hey, my Second-Chance bookmark says "It's never too late to change!" So, after 16 years of sinful living, I've decided chastity is the way to go. Just think about it. No more agonizing over who's gonna call first after a one-night stand. No more letting each other's sexual performance colour your true feelings. No more sleeping in the wet spot. From now on, I can use all that wasted sexual energy for more productive things. Like trying to keep my mind off wanting it.

And I'm not talking Donna of "Beverly Hills 90210" virginity, where everything but sticking it in is allowed. Or the involuntary not-getting-any version. This is true-blue (ball) chastity. According to members of the Body & Soul Posse, who take their orders from God, that means no contact that could stir your loins. Because, according to the Big

Guy, when it comes to sexual pleasure, "arousal is spousal." End of story.

"We hug a lot," says 22-year-old Emily, who started the chastity support "Posse" with the help of her mom seven years ago in Philadelphia. Hand-holding is barely tolerated or, if you're feeling particularly temptation-resilient, you might let yourself get really down and dirty and indulge in a light peck on the cheek. No tongue-diving.

"Basically, we say stop at the hug," says Emily, "because sex is a progression, it's not just sexual intercourse. Kissing is the beginning, so we say 'Stop before you even start.'"

Even sexual thoughts are enough to scuttle your filthy butt off to confession. And masturbation is strictly hands off. I'm starting to have second thoughts about my revirginalization.

"How do you do it?" I asked John, desperately. At 22, he's only gone out on two dates before he met Emily and decided she was "the one." They've "known each other" (you're not allowed to call each other boyfriend and girlfriend until you're sure he or she is going to be your altar-mate) for a year-and-a-half. They're getting married in November. They haven't even deep-kissed. Talk about build-up! Looking forward to the wedding night, kids?

"I pray," he tells me. "I do have temptations like any

other person, you just learn to control yourself." And wear steel underwear. Man, that's willpower! I can't even save money. How am I going to save myself?

He and Emily also avoid "single" dating. Instead, members of the 30-strong Posse go out in groups. "There's less pressure and the best way to learn about someone you're interested in is to see how they interact with other people," John tells me. Chastity Club Med.

I'm not so sure the Fear of God is gonna do much for me at this point. I stopped going to church about the same time I lost my first virginity (hmm...) and I haven't been struck down yet.

But God doesn't have to be your only motivation, says Harold Visser of the Canadian Alliance For Chastity (CAFC). At 21, he's never kissed a girl, at least not in that way. But he stresses that's a personal choice, based on his own faith, not necessarily the CAFC line.

The Alliance operates as information central for the handful of chastity organizations that have sprouted up across Canada over the last few years. CAFC tries to stay away from religion, says Visser, and simply impresses on kids that they can make a decision about their own sexuality, that they can set limits and practice "wise dating" until they're ready, not necessarily for marriage, but to make a lifelong commitment to someone.

"When it comes to making out, it tends to take on a life of its own," he says. "We encourage kids to set their limits ahead of time, to recognize that these are desires, not needs." No guff. That's why it's so fun, silly.

"They're having fun but they're also getting hurt," continues Visser. I suppose we should keep them out of the playgrounds then, too. Because, before you know it, someone loses an eye. Or gets pregnant. Or gets sick.

With an estimated 55 percent of teens between the age of 15 and 19 doing it, maybe these folks have a right to be concerned. But abstinence? Let's get real. The last time we tried preaching that was in the 50s, and pregnancy rates were just as high or higher. And everyone knows that the more you tell a teenager not to do something, the more they'll go out of their way to do it.

This is different, Visser insists. "We aren't trying to go back to the days when sex was 'bad' and you weren't supposed to talk about it. We talk about it all the time. And we're not trying to instill guilt or fear, just mutual and self-respect." In some cases, as in his own, he admits, it is a moral decision.

Sort of like the difference between being a vegetarian for health reasons or out of a moral objection to chowin' down on our four-legged friends? Sounds good in theory, but how many times can you walk past the yummy-smelling smoked meat or pastrami shop before you break down and go in?

Visser believes abstinence doesn't get a fair shake in sex-education programs. "We mention that abstinence is the ideal, then dismiss it like, 'it's a nice idea, but forget it because no one can live up to it,' without even explaining it as a lifestyle choice." Maybe that's because some of us have seen how well the "Just say no" campaign has worked in the war against drugs.

Teaching kids self-respect is good but, in the end, negotiating *no* sex seems as complicated, painful, and as difficult as negotiating mature, responsible sex. Only given the nature of us humans, the latter seems a more practical goal.

Besides, I don't think it's merely coincidence that the growth of the chastity movement coincides with the rise of ultra-conservative thinking and a call for the return to traditional family values. Given the fact that this goes hand-in-hand with an anti-abortion, anti-sex education headspace, I'm leery. What happens to the kids who slip? Without the safety net, they're in for a much rougher landing.

As for my new status, all I can say is that God better be ready to come through on that all-forgiving deal he promised. Does grace come in economy size?

Safety Rules

IT'S BEEN SEVERAL YEARS since one of my very closest friends died of AIDS. He was 26, gay, promiscuous—the perfect stereotype of a "high-risk" candidate. We met just as AIDS was rising as a concern. In the few years before he died, he practiced safe sex more than I did. As a heterosexual woman, I wasn't at risk, reeeally, I thought. Women and AIDS wasn't an "issue" yet.

The last time I saw him, he looked like a skeleton with skin, his hollowed-out eyes fading in and out of consciousness. It was the saddest and scariest thing to watch this active, physically fit, totally-hot guy disintegrate before my eyes.

It hit me like a ton of latex. No ad, pamphlet, or health campaign could send the message home quite so clearly. Safer sex was no longer an option. It seemed ludicrous to think it could be for anyone. I was adamant about condom use with all my lovers, whether casual, long-term, or one-night stands. (Believe me, fear does not necessarily curb promiscuity. Let's get real here: if casual sex is a vice, anxiety will only send you seeking more of it.) I didn't give a shit about whether it was proper to discuss "high-risk activity" vs. "high-risk groups." It only takes once, I'd tell my partners, for anybody. If you don't like it, whack off.

But as is always the case, time eased the pain of my loss. The memory of my friend, while still always present, faded along with the fear and urgency I felt about AIDS. For me to sit here and say that I still always practice entirely safe sex would be like saying I've never faked an orgasm.

I'm from a generation that started having sex in the pre-AIDS era. And since we were in just as much denial about STDs, pregnancy was the only "danger" surrounding sex. And the pill took care of that. Regular condoms were *more* of a novelty item than the bells-and-whistles varieties available today.

Habits apparently are more durable than condoms. I won't have condom-less sex with someone I've just met, I don't swallow and wouldn't even consider anal sex without a wrap, but what about vaginal intercourse after the 10th or 20th time with the same person? What about when you slip once and let it go *this* time? If his dick doesn't fall off and world order remains, the condom sometimes doesn't next time. I find myself slacking off, buying into the if-it-hasn't-happened-yet-it-probably-won't-besides-it-won't-happen-to-me school of thought.

AIDS is hardly in the news anymore. When it does make it to the headlines, it becomes like Rwanda, or Bosnia, or any other story that's happening "somewhere else." Unless we're personally affected, we eventually stop paying attention and turn to the comics.

More than a decade into the "crisis" and billions of dollars later, it would seem all we've ended up with is a lot of misinformation, some heightened awareness, but little change in attitudes. AIDS is still primarily viewed as a gay issue.

Ask most straight teens having sex today and condoms still aren't cool, even though these kids have grown up with the fear of AIDS. For many, "Uh yeah, that whole AIDS thing is scary" is about the extent of their discussion on the issue.

Apparently, one in four heterosexual men still doesn't use condoms. Though no one wants to talk about it or admit it (because goodness knows heterosexual men don't need any less incentive to be concerned), most men are aware they're less at risk. Unless they're IV drug-users or screwing men without a condom, it's the women they sleep with who are in danger. That's us, sisters.

I'm aware of the issues. I know what I'm supposed to

do. I'm supposed to be in control, and have developed enough self-esteem to demand respect and be able to negotiate safer sex.

Sometimes, though, I have trouble just simply negotiating sex.

In many ways, AIDS did get us talking about our sexual activities. That was before it started being used as an excuse in the swing back to moral conservatism. It was AIDS that supposedly made us more interested in monogamy, commitment, and marriage.

But for many, that's where the discussion stopped. Now there's little room to discuss our fears and mistakes in between the moral judgments and the political self-righteousness. If we don't buy into the morals, then we're supposed to be able to handle the risks, we're suppose to know better. I do know better, but I still do a lot of things in life I shouldn't. I need more help with that middle ground.

Sex is dangerous, it always has been, physically and psychologically. So is getting in a car. But that doesn't stop anyone from engaging in either activity. What I wanna know is: why is it that, when it comes to my own safety, I never think twice about putting my seatbelt on?

Sex for Sale

Sex Toys 'r' Us

THE GUY NERVOUSLY RESTACKING the boxes of rubber vaginas he had just knocked over was trying to make like he wasn't actually checking out the tower of twats when they toppled. The young, leather-jacketed guy was pretty average-looking, like most of the people shuffling through Seduction last Saturday afternoon. In fact, most of the customers at the city's Walmart of sex shops—5000 square feet of fun—looked like they had stopped in on their way home from the mall.

Honouring sex-shop etiquette, my friend and I avoided any eye-contact with the young couples ("Oh look honey, triple-x videos are on special this week, two for $30!"), suburban rockers, and other assorted sex-crazed folks fingering the racks of tacky, badly-made lingerie, the aisles and aisles of dildos, rubber dolls, lotions, oils, and genital-shaped everything lining the shelves. ("Penis-shaped salt & pepper shakers, just what I've been looking for.")

We weren't sure what we were looking for and you know that old saying, "Never shop on an empty stomach." But rather than succumb to my urge ("Grab a cart, honey!"), we tried to be practical. ("Now dear, do you really need gold lamé boxers?")

We decided a dildo would be fun. My last one got lost in the settlement of a former relationship. There must have been 200 varieties of the things, all lined up, staring erectly at me on those sex supermarket shelves. "Life-like" is apparently a big selling point, the veinier the better. I personally favour the smooth, hard-plastic models. I'd rather have a toy I know is a toy. Pretending it's the real thing when it's moulded plastic is rather disturbing and a bit depressing.

Did I mention variety? There were finger-slim dildos, "Monster Dongs," strap-on dildos, and dildos with little elephants perched on top whose ivories do the tickling while a slim pencil-like piece of plastic provides for personal two-way pleasure. Holy goose!

The glow-in-the-dark model, I figured, might come in handy if you're doing it in the closet, or maybe you prefer the gold "disco dildo" for more festive occasions. Even the neon trend didn't escape the dildo designers.

I suppose the handy purse-size dildo would do the trick if the need suddenly arose, say if you were on the bus, or at the laundromat. And the remote-control model would allow you to be discreet about it. "That humming noise? I really don't know what it is either, sir." (Also handy if your guy's a hopeless channel surfer. Just slip him the vibro-control, he'll never know the difference.)

There was a travel kit for those who are coming *and* going, while the most elaborate models came with more attachments than my mother's Filter Queen. When I finally caught up with the plastic "tickler" attachment I had sent bouncing across the tile floor, I bent over to pick it up, and my eyes were greeted with what looked like something my father used to milk the cows back on our farm. I was in the "Men's" department. Apparently, some guys use the huge plastic cylinder attached to the rubber tube, attached to the pressure gauge, to get off. This was some pretty serious "hard" ware. The penis pumps seemed more suited to the garage than the bedroom. These too came in quite a variety, holding promises of bigger and better things or simply the best wank you'll come across. The plastic life-like mould of porn-queen Barbara Dare's vagina (officially supervised by Dare herself) was more than a little disturbing. So were the blow-up dolls, with their gaping, vibrating mouths. I knew it was time to move on when I saw one that claimed to hold up to 300 pounds and sold for $160. The image it conjured up was a bit hard to take. Feeling somewhat misrepresented and out of sorts, I was anxious to get back to the dildos—I took them less personally.

We finally settled on a smooth, slim, black (it goes with everything) plastic vibrator and thought maybe some exotic oil would be a nice treat. Again, the selection was slightly overwhelming with every colour and flavour imaginable at your fingertips. While I appreciated the efforts to make our lovemaking as sweet and savoury as possible, licking gobs of tutti-frutti off my partner brought back memories of eating too much Halloween candy as a kid. We were just about to settle on a simple concoction that looked a little less tacky than the rest when I checked out the ingredients: coconut oil, vegetable oil, and some artificial edible ingredients. At 14 bucks for a tiny bottle, I figured we'd be just as well off sticking to the Crisco in the cupboard at home. We settled on a trial size of Wet lube.

Obviously, there is a definite vested interest in keeping this stuff taboo. How else could they get away with charging $60 for a crappy vinyl harness, or $40 for a skin mag wrapped in plastic so you don't even know what you're getting? Thank God for honest help. It saved me from shelling out $18 to find out if Spanish Fly really works. It doesn't, I was told.

Beyond the rip-off factor, the mixed feeling of wanting to run screaming from the store in disgust and wanting to fill up a shopping cart with all the stuff you're curious about, and the fear that your mother will somehow come strolling by just as you're walking out the door of the place, it's really quite a blast. Especially going as a couple. You get to explore each other's taste, and not just in body goop. And then you get to enjoy the best part of buying new toys; rushing home to play with them.

Mind Games

I'M LOOKING AT AN IMAGE in *Penthouse*. It's a "guy/chick" shoot that is supposed to be focused on her pleasure. Her pout doesn't convince me, but him lapping up the champagne she is pouring over her crotch excites me.

And bugs me. I'm not supposed to like it. Sometimes, I don't. My feelings range from anger to just thinking it looks tacky and ridiculous. But sometimes, I get off on it. Maybe I harbour a deep-seated desire to have four-inch long nails, big hair, and to wear stilettos and tacky lingerie. Maybe I'm just as duped as the guys who believe this is sexy.

Fantasy often doesn't make much sense.

I won't tolerate violence against women but I can fantasize about being tied up and taken by force. I may be in a happy, monogamous relationship but I get turned on by the idea of sex with someone else. I don't consider myself an exhibitionist but I might get off on the idea of doing it in a public place. I consider myself straight but I fantasize about going down on a woman.

But that's what fantasy is for. "Fantasizing" about what our lives, or we, are not. They're a bit like dreams. We have little control over them, and sometimes they leave you in a sweat. The thing with dreams is that, even though some of them feel really real, we know they're not. When we're dealing with sexual fantasy we're less comfortable with this line. Weird dreams make us go, "wow, that was weird." Weird fantasies make us nervous.

It's hard to say where our fantasies come from. Maybe they have something to do with desiring what we can't have. Maybe they come from some internal neurosis that our mind is trying to work out. Maybe they're just something to keep us amused.

One thing that does define fantasy is that it is *not* reality. I may fantasize about being raped, but that certainly doesn't mean that I would ever want it to happen. Like our dreams, fantasies tap into our subconscious and go wild even if we don't. But we're in the driver's seat. That's the beauty of it.

Fantasizing about someone lapping champagne from my loins is pretty darned exciting, I have to admit. But whether I do it or not is up to me. I'm in control. I decide where it goes, whether I like it just fine up there in my head, whether I want to share it, or whether I want to indulge in it, I make the call.

In a story in *Playgirl*, a woman meets a masked stranger at a masquerade party. He forces her to have sex with him on the balcony while the party carries on inside. She gets into it.

If this were to actually happen to me, I would probably be horrified, so why does reading it, in the safety of my home, or with a partner, turn me on?

The woman in the story is not in control, but as a reader, I am. If I decide to tell my partner that I'm turned on by the idea of being forced to have sex, I'll only do it if I am sure that he knows he should never do this against my will.

I'm reading Anaïs Nin's *Delta of Venus*. One of the stories is about a baron who encourages his young daughters to come into his room in the morning and jump around on his bed and grab his "finger" as it moves around under the sheets while he secretly gets off.

Sometimes when I read this story it grosses me out, but sometimes I get off, and sometimes the fact that I get off pisses me off.

Fantasies are a bit nuts that way. It's tough to explain to your mate why you have a secret desire to dress up like a lumberjack during sex, so better not to say anything at all.

So then we all walk around feeling like our fantasies are weirder than everyone else's. And no one says anything.

But we all have them. Some are weirder than others and some people have a harder time distinguishing them from reality. But most of us don't. We just have them—all the time. Fantasy is crucial. It taps into all the grey areas. Instead of feeling like a weirdo, feeling okay about whatever I may fantasize about allows me to explore my fears and inhibitions.

And they make the work day fly by.

Porn Stars

THERE I WAS, IN A ROOM with some 500 academics, therapists, and educators, watching porn videos on a huge screen at the front of the auditorium.

Context is everything, right? I mean, really, the only thing that made this different from, say, catching a flick at Cinéma L'Amour was that the screen was larger, and we were watching in the name of research, part of a quest for a deeper understanding of sex—this, and the fact that the videos on the screen were those of "feminist pornographer" (no, it's not an oxymoron) Candida Royalle.

Royalle was the keynote speaker on the second evening of a sexuality conference I was attending. Eight hundred people from all over the continent talking about sex for three days.

So there I was, amongst a pretty straight-laced congregation squirming in their seats while larger-than-life men and women got naked and licked, sucked, and fucked in front of us. True to the genre, the videos were rife with less than academy award-winning performances, cheesy music, and bad lighting. What distinguished Royalle's videos was the notable absence of, as she puts it, "piston action and cum shots."

Royalle, a porn-video star in the 70s, left her "acting" career, spent eight years in therapy pitting her feminist politics against her former career choice, and, much to her surprise, the whole process landed her back where she started —but this time, on the other side of the camera.

In an industry where everyone told her women didn't like porn, Royalle insisted this was only because existing porn didn't like women. She was determined to make up for the lack of pleasure-oriented material for females. In 1984, Royalle started her own company, Femme Distribution Inc., producing videos aimed at "average" heterosexual couples, a market she was certain existed. Ten years and as many titles later, Royalle has proven her point.

Femme's catalogue describes its products as "erotic films for the woman who knows what she wants and the men who love her." A nice change from the usual "Skin flicks for men to guiltily wank off to when no one is around and the curtains are drawn." As Royalle says, "When I started working in porn in the 70s, these movies were only shown in dark little theatres. And I thought, if the guys who go into these theatres think this is what sex is about—that this is how you make love to a woman—then it's no wonder they have to sit in a dark theater by themselves."

Royal says she tries to focus less on genitalia and intercourse in her films, and instead emphasizes build-up, anticipation, and playfulness. I personally found them a bit tame and, at least in the clips we saw, still pretty conventional orifice-oriented sex. But, judging by the crush of women and men who surrounded her after the screening wanting to know where they could get copies of her vids in Canada (for academic purposes, of course), her approach is appreciated.

Admittedly, I have watched many a porn video in frustration, fast-forwarding my way through the misogyny and the tackiness, reconciling the heat in my pants with the boiling of my blood. Royalle's is a welcome alternative.

Obnoxious porn isn't going to go away any time soon; it's too huge an industry. It's quite obvious that even Royalle, slick, articulate, and full of marketing savvy, is in this to make money. But at least she's female-sex positive and politically aware. While I have no illusions that this is an industry selling pleasure to those willing to pay for it, I'm glad to see some women stepping in to respond to consumer demand, smashing the old-boy monopoly on exploitative fantasy.

Royalle has developed a support network of women like herself, former dancers and porn-video stars, who are now producing their own girl-positive stuff. People like Annie Sprinkle, Fanny Fatale, Veronica Veer, Gloria Leonard, and Veronica Hart. These are strong women, Royalle insists, nothing like the stereotype of sex-trade workers as sexually abused, messed-up girls with no self-respect and nowhere to go.

An article in *Playboy* (I just read it for the articles) about women in the porn industry included Lily Braindrop, the editor of *Taste of Latex*, a 'zine out of San Francisco which describes itself as "Entertainment for the sexually disenfranchised." She calls herself the "champion of the sexual underdogs," and describes conventional male porn as "the bastard child of the soul."

The article also described The Lusty Lady, a peepshow in San Francisco, run by Catherine Bedel, an ex-dancer and single mother with an MBA from Berkeley. The club serves a primarily male clientele, but Bedel at least tries to hire women who challenge the preconceived ideology of an erotic performer. She also guarantees a wage to the dancers, as well as providing an unlimited supply of toilet paper and tampons. Now there's someone after a girl's heart.

Debra Sundahl publishes *On Our Backs*, a lesbian-focused erotic magazine, and produces and directs erotic videos through her own production company, Fatale Videos.

The list goes on… these women are leading an erotic revolution of sorts and, from the centre of my pleasure, I salute them.

Virtual Virgin

IT WAS MY FIRST TIME. I couldn't wait any longer. Sure, it probably would have been better in more intimate surroundings, perhaps in the comfort of my own home. And yes, I would have loved to share the experience with someone I love, someone whose equipment I was familiar with. Instead, I had to settle for someone who simply had the equipment and was willing to show it to me. I chose my colleague Matt. He seemed the most experienced and familiar with the way it all worked.

We did it in the office, on a Saturday afternoon, when no one else was around. I wanted to try some of the real raunchy stuff right off the bat. Matt was a little hesitant, but since it was my first time, I could tell he was eager to make it a memorable experience.

Once we connected, Matt showed me his BBS. (A BBS or electronic Bulletin Board Service is like a package of selections from across the great Internet divide that are made available to users for a monthly fee.) There we found alt.binaries.pictures.erotica. The list of available images ranged from amateur to bestiality, bondage, and softcore Japanese animation stills. While intrigued by best. hamster.duct.tape, I opted for best.woman.horse (growing up on a farm and all, ya know). Let me tell you, that woman was doing things to that horse, I never saw back home. Yow! What an initiation. Trust me, you don't even wanna know what we found in the sex.shit file. Hot lunch, anyone? It was time to get outta there.

After that little expansion of horizons, we came across something even scarier while surfing the weird and wonderful sexual underworld of the Internet. Just past the Anna Nicole Smith House of Worship and right next to alt.sex.erotica.pictures.necrophilia was alt.sex. erotica. pictures.Marsha Clark. I'll never be able to watch the O.J. trial the same way.

A lot of the guys (considering the content and estimates that 95 percent of Net users are male, it's a pretty safe guess) who post these images (I'd like to talk to their mothers) have nifty Net stage names like Scanboy, who posted pictures of "chicks with willies," or Puffy, who decided he'd like to share his stock pile of Tracie Lord nudies.

In the true interactive spirit of the Net, people post requests for pictures too. (There are guys who still get woodies over Vanna White!?) Much more hip was a request for shots of Gates McFadden's hips. (*Star Trek: The Next Generation's* Dr. Beverly Crusher, for those of you who aren't from here.)

Pictures needn't just be of public personalities. Kayla from Oregon decided to post naked pictures of herself along with her phone number and address. Now that's what I call direct marketing. If you're camera shy, you can always share what you sound like in the sack. That's what Sandy did in Alt.sex.erotica.sound.11part.Sandy. Heck, if you listened to Sandy and looked at Kayla, it'd almost be the real thing.

Aside from photos, sound, and video (we didn't have the software to check out video), you can also get off on good old-fashioned dirty talk. Text sex newsgroups range from things like the seven-part sex story we came across (boring!) to conferences where people engage in discussions on important sexual matters, as in alt.sex.fetish.diapers.

About this time, I was ready for some live action. Matt hooked me into an IRC, an Internet Relay Chat. This is where people chat back and forth on-line in real time about all kinds of stuff. Of course, as we know, get five people in a room and they'll eventually start talking about sex. Get 30 million people on a net, same principle. The added bonus here is that it's relatively anonymous.

I chose the "Let's fuck" chat group. I liked its directness

and, besides, it was the only one that had more than one or two people on it.

What a let-down. This group certainly didn't live up to its name. I tried, but these folks were all over the place. C'mon kids, focus! Some of our West-Coast participants complained that it was still a little early in the morning for any serious hot talk. But the biggest problem I found was the delay factor. By the time Shapeman typed in his reply to my direct offer, Da Mask and Kate had a whole other conversation going on. Thanks to my grade-nine typing skills, I managed to get in on the chat enough to pique some interest. (It helps being a girl. From what I hear, Net users tend to zoom in on anything that looks even vaguely female.) But as soon as I finally had Shapeman convinced to sneak off with me into our own private chat room, our computer decided to call it quits.

Not bad for my first time. Of course, when you look at the possibilities out there, Matt and I barely made it to first base. I'm intrigued enough to go further and have only begun to grasp the complex issues and opportunities this new medium presents.

Obviously, the Net is about a lot more than sex, but there's no denying, as Da Mask told me during our chat, "Alt.sexgroups, that's where the crowd is." It may be a new medium but it's the same human nature behind the keyboard. Also not new, when it comes to sex, quantity doesn't equal quality. I mean, how many people want to read someone's seven-part badly written sexual fantasy? As for the really outrageous-sounding stuff; a lot of it doesn't live up to its provocative filename. And sometimes the file literally comes up empty.

In some ways, if you boiled down the true sexual content on the Net, you'd probably get a cross-section that was no more disturbing than what is available at your local adult magazine or video store.

Mind you, I have to admit that while I might let my curiosity get the best of me while sitting in front of the computer in the privacy of my own home, I'd be less inclined to walk into a porn shop and asking them to direct me to the horse-dong titles.

Body Signs

RECENTLY, the Quebec Court of Appeal ruled that a bylaw prohibiting sex club owners from putting up signs depicting nudity outside their clubs was a nasty violation of freedom of expression.

Hurray for the constitutional lawyers. They saw it as a great victory for our civil liberties and freedom.

Hurray for the club owners. They can continue to exercise their right to make money, ahem, I mean to freedom of expression.

Hurray for Montreal. We get to continue drawing tourists to our sexy city with all its titillating attractions.

Hurray for the women who work in these clubs. They get to keep their well paying, stimulating jobs.

Hurray for the consumers (read, stupid men). They get to keep forking over heaps of cash to get women to take their clothes off.

Ahhh, democracy, such a well-oiled machine.

Yeah, I know, banning these signs would set a dangerous precedent and would do little to deal with why they exist in the first place. I know that if they were gone, it's not as if I could stroll downtown feeling victorious, having eradicated the exploitation of women by freeing our landscape of tacky depictions of female bodies.

And personally, I can't say I feel "degraded" when I look at these signs. The most I can work up is a groan or maybe an exasperated sigh. But what about the women they advertise?

Teresa used to be amused by the signs outside these clubs. Now they make her feel sick to her stomach. She was a dancer for three months. She had been working in a regular bar to put herself through university. A friend who worked as a dancer pointed out that she had been doing the same thing—"working in a bar putting up with assholes"—and making a hell of a lot more money for it. It seemed like sound logic.

Teresa loved it at first. She loved dancing and the stage. "I was insecure about my body. It made me feel validated. People paid me to be naked; they thought I looked that good."

Pretty soon, though, Teresa found she had to get drunk or high just to stay at work. Men grabbing her, touching her, wanting to shove broken beer bottles up her butt got to her. She realized how many of these women did it to keep themselves or their boyfriends in drugs or their kids in food. She started feeling controlled by it. "I needed the money for school, for a computer, but I started feeling disassociated from my body. I'd be fondling myself on stage and feel dead.

"Then I realized, sure I can take it, anyone can take a certain amount of abuse if they have to, or are used to it, or don't realize other options." Teresa realized her option and left. She spent all the money she saved on a two-week drinking binge and started bussing tables at a restaurant.

Tracy has another take. She's been dancing for two years, and has no problem with the idea that men come and pay money to watch her take her clothes off. "A lot of these guys are just lonely and want a pretty girl to talk to and they're willing to pay for it," she says. As far as the signs go, she brings it down to basics: more customers means more money. And the pictures bring people into the club. Hurray for the free market.

"These women are beautiful or they have 40-inch busts to advertise," says Tracy. "Take Tiffany Towers. She's got boobs that aren't even normal, and when these young guys see her picture they go, 'wow! Look at that; let's check it out.'"

Some cities have big nickels, we have big breasts. Well, if Tiffany Towers is doing well by her "talents" then so be it.

I'm not about to change that by taking down her picture. And I'm sure Tiffany Towers wouldn't exactly appreciate it if I did. Or maybe she would. I don't know Tiffany or what she thinks of her job.

Tracy also started dancing when she was waitressing and met a friend making $300 a night as a dancer. At 21, Tracy says dancing is not her choice career, "but the money's good and it's better than working at McDonald's.

"The truth of the matter is that there's only so much money you can make as a woman and there's not many jobs that offer this kind of money," says Teresa. "If these women are into it, I'm not going to tell them to go work as a receptionist for next to nothing for hard, boring work."

And, if these clubs feel they have a constitutional right to express to the world that they have really bad graphic designers, fine. I'm just as ready to pat our justice system on the back and claim victory for freedom of ideas. (Oddly, our courts don't show the same zeal when it comes to stopping censorship of lesbian or gay erotica.)

It's obvious that money talks, and as long as these clubs are so profitable, they will always be able to hire someone to fight for their right to make money. If this is seen as a victory for freedom of expression, great. We should take advantage of it as a chance to push for the same rights in other areas, ones that will move us toward a more equal society, where women have more financial options and where everyone enjoys the same freedoms to express themselves. Not just those who like big breasts.

Me and the Girls

Table Talk

A WOMAN'S PLACE is definitely in the kitchen. But only if you're there with a bunch of other women, sitting around the kitchen table drinking too much coffee or cheap wine, smoking each other's cigarettes, eating junk food, and discussing important world matters. Like who's cuter, Johnny Depp or Brad Pitt?

Girlfriends and kitchen tables are a necessity in my life. It is here where life crises, bad relationships, and bad hair are debated and discussed at length. When it's me and the girls in our 50s, I'm sure we'll still be sitting around the kitchen table discussing everything from gender politics to preserving (you should hear my friend's comparative analysis of pickles and penises), and holding regular deep-throat banana contests.

I need this. Most women I know need this. I know that when I'm losing it, when work/personal life/the future sucks, all someone has to do is yell BRUNCH!!! and I know everything is gonna be OK. I pack my stress and a bottle of Bordeaux and head over to hang in a friend's kitchen. Sitting around with four or five close girlfriends, suddenly the world seems a better place. I feel important and connected. Self-consciousness drops away, insecurities are left at the door or heaped on the table before us to be scrutinized, dissected, laughed at, and eventually tossed aside. Then we eat.

We gush over each other, reaffirm how wonderful we all are, offer advice, consolation, and share the quality of orgasms we've been achieving as of late. Yes, we nurture one another.

And we laugh. A lot.

I used to think I would never be happy in a relationship with a man unless I could have the same intense closeness I share with my girlfriends. Unless we could lie around, try each other's clothes on while discussing yeast infections, it would never work, I thought. Until I finally accepted that most men can't appreciate good yeast-infected humour anyway. They'd be mortally wounded to know that when you're cooing, "Oh yes, over there harder, harder, little to the left, little to the right, hmmm... that's it!" you're not actually getting off but using them as a human scratching post.

No, I'm feeling a lot more selfish about my female friendships these days. No matter how sensitive and in touch with their feelings men become, I can't see them ever exchanging muff-diving tips or revealing how self-conscious they are about their zitty backs. Most guys wouldn't be caught dead exposing themselves in a group of peers. Maybe one on one, and even then, it's usually rather cryptic. "I'm really fucked up, wanna go shoot some pool?" Male bonding at its finest.

It's not that they don't want to. Most just can't. Revealing their secret self goes against everything they're taught. It may mean they go through life feeling a bit more lonely or disconnected, but compared to the terror of tapping into that part of themselves, it apparently seems a small price to pay. Hockey scores are much simpler to keep track of. And there is always work.

Ah work, the evil plot to undermine female bonding. While we are all running around overachieving to impress the boys, our girl time is being seriously cut into. We work in male environments where this kind of camaraderie is discouraged or seen as unproductive or wasting time. Between work, time for myself, a relationship, and maybe some sleep, I find myself exhausted. I lose touch. I need my girlfriends. As a temporary measure, Ma Bell lets me reach out and touch someone, but eventually I need the real thing. This is usually the point where I run out of the office screaming "GIRL NIGHT!!!"

Yes, like my favourite soap opera, I may not manage to see my girlfriends for long stretches at a time. But luckily, it only takes one episode to catch up.

Cover Girls

IT'S TIME FOR ME to face the truth. I have a problem.

It used to be a novelty, a social activity, something to enjoy among friends.

Now I find myself doing it alone in the privacy of my own home, at all times of the day. And once I get a taste, I can't stop, I want more.

I never used to buy my own. I relied on other people's stash, or just stuff I'd find lying around. Occasionally, I'd allow myself to check out what was available. But soon, this wasn't enough.

Now I'm left with the guilt of having squandered hard-earned money to support my habit. When the financial guilt is too much, I resort to stealing to satisfy my cravings; lurking around laundromats and waiting rooms perusing the goods, slipping them under my arm and making a smooth, undetected escape.

Yes, it's true, I'm a women's magazine junkie.

My Messy Bedroom

Fashion mags, beauty bibles, trash, mindless drivel, whatever you want to call them, I can't get enough.

I know it's a crutch, a substitute, that I'm running away from the truth, from my real self, but I can't help it. I'm seduced by the promise of quick, easy solutions to all my inadequacies: my insensitive man, my inability to meet my potential, my inner thighs.

In my desperate search for at least one article that will tell me something I don't already know, while every all-encompassing headline seduces me with answers to all that ails me and fails me, a moment of sobriety takes hold.

Standing in the news-stand, eyes as glossed-over as the sea of magazine covers before me, I stop and wonder what it is that makes me want to pick up *Mademoiselle* and not *Maclean's*, *New Woman* before *Newsweek*. Am I so shallow and frivolous? But I'm a feminist. How can this be?

I know I'm not the only one. There are more of you out there, admit it, girls. Sitting around suffering pangs of guilt for literally buying into society's expectations, meanwhile devouring them in all their contradictions. What is it we love about finding an article that promises "Knowing Yourself, a Step-by-Step Path to Inner Happiness" right next to "Thinner Thighs in 30 days (Without Dieting)"? It's funny, yeah, but, c'mon, it does tap into our psyche. Even if we hate to admit it.

Is it the wanna-be in us, that self-worth destroying, if-only-I-could-look-like-her feeling? I don't think so. I'd like to think I got over that. I don't necessarily desire cleavage I can bury my nose in.

Maybe it's my mother's fault. She raised me on *Chatelaine* and *Women's World*.

Maybe it's that they are all about us. Okay, so they're not *really* about us—or anyone we know for that matter—but they're the only mainstream media devoted exclusively to *trying* to be about us.

Then again, who can resist promises of money, perpetual happiness in life and love, and a great bod to boot? And let's talk about sex. A random sampling of one month's offerings alone includes "Kinky Things You Can Do to Make Him Last Longer in Bed," "My Night With a Gigolo," "Sexual Clues That Say He'll Commit (No Matter What He Says or Does)," "Love, Sex, and Marriage in the 90s," "Love & Temptation," "Love Slaves: When Every Romance Becomes an Obsession," "Endless Love: How You Can Make Love Last a Lifetime," and " Wives Who Cheat and Risk Their Good Marriages for Great Sex."

Guys aren't immune. I catch them casually flipping through these mags when no one is looking. They get seduced too; they're just not allowed to admit it. Most guys are dying to know what we're interested in and, more importantly, what we're saying about them. Of course, the information is usually as relevant to them as the stuff about us is to us. Hey boys, did you know that your bedroom decor tells us everything we need to know about you?

The substance (or lack thereof) of these magazines is restricted to "girl stuff." Trashy mags are about stuff most women like to talk about: relationships, fashion, our insecurities, how to have better skin. I think that's cool.

I feel oddly safe in their contradictions, their feminist leanings ("Never Married and Glad of It!"), and their insistence on leanness. Maybe that's because these contradictions are, in some ways, a reflection of where woman are at these days. "I want to make it to the top and damn it, my lipstick's gonna be perfect when I get there!"

Separation anxiety with my former teen self? Fear of moving on? Or of completely living by all the rules I've made for myself as an "independent woman?" Escapism? Avoidance? Consumerism? Whatever it is, I'm hooked.

Sure, I can quit anytime.

But you know what they say. You really have to want to quit. At least that's what I read in a trashy women's mag somewhere, once.

Booby Trap

THEE LINGERIE SHOPPE on Hamilton St. in Regina, Saskatchewan is like a refuge. Owners Laurette Bell and Louise Trudelle care about breasts. They made mine feel special and unique as they lovingly wiggled them into some of the best-fitting and most beautiful bras I've ever seen.

And these women know their titties. Trained in breast anatomy, they have been fitting bras the old-fashioned way for years. No off-the-rack shopping here. Each customer gets individual attention: after carefully sizing you up, they bring you bra after bra until you get the right fit.

Women from across Canada and the U.S., come to this shop because they import sizes and styles domestic manufacturers don't make. Reginians take visiting guests to the local museum, the RCMP headquarters, and Thee Lingerie Shoppe.

The store keeps files on every woman they fit, following some women's growth from pubescent sprouting (Forget training bras, these women insist. They're just a cover-up; they're not training anything.) right through adulthood.

I'm on file as a 34-D.

I was shocked when they told me. A D-cup! That was what my rather well-endowed mother might wear, but not me. Impossible. I had long taken comfort in the fact that I fit into that supposedly average, and so popular 36-C.

A good friend, originally from Regina, was the one to get me to Thee Lingerie Shoppe. She insisted I had a bra problem. She had already experienced the life-altering experience of discovering a well-fitted bra. A size 8 who wears a 32-DD bra, she has endured years of department store salesclerks insisting they "had nothing pretty in that size, dear," or immediately handing her a size 38 as soon as she announced her cup size.

Still I wasn't quite convinced and, in fact, more than a little annoyed at her insistence that I was so incapable of cupping my own breasts. After all, it was the second such trauma of my life.

It was in grade nine that my best friend boldly insisted that I should start wearing a bra. I felt so clueless as I looked down at the budding protrusions in my T-shirt. She lent me one of hers. It was a Dici. Remember those flimsy crossover ones with the frontal closure? Louise and Laurette would have been appalled.

But it was true. Once I got that 34-D on, I was a changed person. I stood up straighter, my clothes fit better, and the damn thing wasn't always riding up my back or slipping off my shoulders all the time.

I have now joined my friend in her crusade to get women into good bras. Sure, there may be more important causes to fight, but don't be fooled. This is serious stuff.

Beyond the annoying slipping and riding, there are grave side-effects for women who carry an extra burden throughout life without proper support. Louise and Laurette have seen it all. Rounded shoulders, humped backs, women who've had to have shoulder operations because an ill-fitted bra was making the straps do all the heavy-lifting, when it should be done by the back of the bra.

In one case, they said, a woman had open flesh wounds between her breasts. She came into the store in tears because her doctor told her she would have to have surgery to correct it. Louise and Laurette got her in the right bra size, one that allowed her breasts to breath, and things healed up. The woman had been wearing a 40-B, she was a 36-FF.

According to Bell, the problem began when bras became self-serve in the late 40s. We've now had a few generations of women who've been buying their bras off-the-rack and we no longer know how a bra should fit. We tend to increase the size (if a 34-B doesn't fit, we go up to 36 or 38) before we increase the cup size. But, if you tell women they need a D or larger cup, they scoff "I'm not that big." Meanwhile, they'll insist they wear a size 36-C bra, even though, according to Laurette, while this has become the ideal measurement, it actually applies to someone who would probably need a size-14 dress. Not so ideal. All of this might explain why you want to run screaming from the hideous fluorescent-lit dressing room after you've tried on what seems like a million bras and not one of them looks anything like they do in the picture on the box.

And it's not just the well-endowed who have this problem. For example, one broad-backed, small-breasted friend of mine tries on small cupped bras which rarely come larger than 36 inches around. The cups end up in the middle of her chest with her boobs squeezed east and west.

Needless to say, bra sizes are as individual as shoe sizes. And most of us wear our bras for at least as long as our shoes every day. Of course, no one would dispute the importance of a good-fitting pair of shoes.

So now we're stuck in a vicious circle. We're all buying the wrong size bras either because we don't know any better or we want to fit into the current fashion trend. Stores pass this information on to their buyers who then tell the manufacturers to keep making lots more of these wrong sizes. And we keep buying them.

And apparently Canada is the worst. Our relatively small market limits the size range even more. Most of our bras start at size 34 and many stop at a C cup. Meanwhile, European and American styles come in D, DD, F, FF, G, and now they even have an H cup.

Confused? Not to worry, you're not the only one. The public relations officer for Canadelle, Canada's largest bra manufacturing and design company, says the biggest complaint she gets from women is that they don't know how a bra is supposed to fit. As a result, the company has designed its first fitting guide.

My friend, the 32-DD, and I see it as a small victory, another step towards freeing women from this booby trap.

Boob Job

SARAH'S OPERATION was first thing the next morning, but I still didn't feel ready. I'd thought long and hard about her decision, but I just couldn't be sure it was the right thing. It seemed so drastic. Having your breastss cut open and their insides gutted like a codfish.

Wasn't this against everything feminism had taught me? We're supposed to be learning to love our bodies, dealing with whatever we've been dealt. So Sarah had big boobs. She just needed to learn to accept them, to recognize and reclaim their power. How could I let her have them lopped in half?

When I first met Sarah, her boobs, as usual, were the centre of attention. When she told me she was planning to have a breast reduction, I, like so many before me, felt the urgent need to set her straight. Armed with my assumptions, I decided she must be really insecure about her body. Obviously she's superficial, obsessed and, being the good-bra advocate that I am, I was sure most of her problems could be solved with the right cup. After all, her boobs didn't seem *that* big.

But Sarah's breasts had always encouraged strong, mostly unsolicited, opinions. "Nice big gazongas!" is foremost in her mind amid the enlightened commentary she has received. It's an odd thing with breasts. Once they're a certain size, they become public property and total strangers feel perfectly okay about letting you know what they think of them. After a while, they take on a life of their own, and the attached person is left playing second fiddle. In fact, Sarah would often find people engrossed exclusively in conversation with them. "Uh, excuse me. Hello! I'm up here.

"I *was* my boobs," Sarah told me. "I know they weren't that enormous, but the way I felt inside was that they were the only thing people would see. There was this obsession with my breasts and my cleavage.

"It's not a disability but it can be very disabling," she said.

Especially when you want to run and play like all the other kids. "When I tried to do aerobics, I'd stop jumping, and they'd still be moving."

In fact, beyond all the undesirable attention, the physical problems associated with large breasts are numerous. Plastic surgeon E. Patricia Egerszegi says neck pain, back pain, bra straps digging into women's shoulders, trouble running, headaches, and difficulty finding clothes that fit, are among the complaints she hears. One large-breasted friend of mine can attest to the last problem. When she was growing up and out, her mother used to switch swimsuit tops and bottoms when the sales person wasn't looking.

But determining whether a woman is doing this for the right reasons can be a tough call, Dr. Egerszegi admits. "You don't want to do them for the wrong reasons. You don't want them to think this is going to solve their job situation or save their marriage," she told me.

In fact, Sarah first approached her GP about having a reduction five years ago, but her doctor discouraged her. "She felt like I was doing it because I didn't like my body."

Five years and much thought and harassment later, Sarah still wanted to do it. She had heard nothing but positive feedback from women who had had reductions. Mammary-challenged women would tell her how lucky she was and that she was crazy to do this. "I'd tell them, 'Strap two cantaloupes to your chest and go around like that for 30 years.'" As for the men, Sarah told me, "It was a sexual thing, it's not like my breasts made me a nicer person." As TV's Roseanne, herself a breast-reductee, put it, "If guys were really more interested in our minds they'd have as many names for them and they'd be having Wet Hat contests in all those bars."

Even the government has an official opinion as to what constitutes too big when it comes to women's breasts. Medicare will foot the bill, but only if you lop off at least 250 grams per boob. That's like a coupla Quarter Pounders a side.

That was no problem in Sarah's case. They got a pound each outta her. When I went to visit her in the hospital after the operation, you could still see the purple-marker blueprints the doctor used as a guide. The thought of the actual operation still makes her gag.

It was scary, she admits. "I was afraid something could go wrong, that it'd make me even freakier than before." She was also worried that she wouldn't be able to breast-feed.

According to Dr. Egerszegi, other possible complications include decreased sensitivity, ugly scars, lumpy breasts, and blood clots. Sometimes part or even all of the nipple—which has to be completely removed and then sewn back on in some cases—actually dies.

So far, Sarah hasn't experienced any problems. When I finally saw her new friends, they looked great, downright perky. "We smile at each other every morning," Sarah laughed.

She's happy with her new look. "I'm excited about having my boobs move with me instead of ahead of me."

Raggin' Out

I REMEMBER COMING HOME from school the day I got my period. I was very excited. I was a bit of a tomboy and everyone in our "group" expected me to get it last. I told my Mom after supper, while doing the dishes. "Guess what happened to me today," I said, feeling nervous and excited. "I got my period!"

"I don't get mine, anymore." After her eighth kid, me, her doctor had insisted on a hysterectomy. "You'll have to talk to your sister."

"Oh," I replied, that sinking feeling creeping right down into my now fertile loins; I suddenly didn't feel so smug about my stained underwear.

My sister handed me a super-monster-jumbo tampon, and left the room. I managed to get it in about halfway and spent the night uncomfortably shifting my butt around wondering if it was supposed to feel so rotten.

What a send-off. Now I was a woman. Hmm... If it hadn't

been for that wonderful little book, *Once a Month an Egg Travels*, that my mother silently handed me one day, I wouldn't have had any idea what was really going on. That, and what my friend told me behind the garage that day. "My dad does what to my mom?!"

It finally dawned on me what all those ambiguous billowy white TV commercials were for. (Little girls today must grow up thinking their periods are gonna be blue.) I used to sneak through the fields to the one store in our village to buy tampons because I got the message loud and clear that no one else in my family wanted to know about my period or deal with it.

Surely things have changed, at least for little girls today whose moms have learned to be a little more comfortable with the whole body change thing. My mother came from a very traditional Catholic upbringing. She was also 40 years older than me. She wasn't very comfortable with that stuff.

Socially, however, this thing that we put up with once a month for more than half of our lives (seven days x 12 months x 40 years + extra for PMS, post-MS, spotting, and ovulation pangs = a lot) is still taboo.

We may have come a little way from the days of viewing menstruating women as unclean or ill. The belief that menstrual blood was dangerous, unlucky, and dirty was useful in keeping women out of sight, out of commission at least once a month. Still, I don't know how many times my moods or reactions have been written off because "it must be that time of the month" or how many times, when I'm really experiencing "that time of the month" in a bad way, I have been made to feel like I've got a convenient excuse.

Our euphemistic approach is more proof of social discomfort with menstruation. Talking about "being on the rag" or "the curse" or your "little friend" makes it even more confusing for young women. My personal favourite, however, is a British term I came across: "jam butties." A butty is British slang for a sandwich. Now that's nice. What a way to make you feel good and gross.

I wish we'd learn to celebrate menarche, as some cultures do. A friend of mine's three-year-old often talks about all the people she's gonna invite to her "period party." Sounds like they've got the right idea.

One last gripe. Who came up with the term "feminine protection" anyway? No doubt, the same dweebs who design the stuff and come up with the brand-names. Satin Touch? I mean, really, it makes having your period sound almost orgasmic. Faced with a wall of wings, super-absorbent, day-time, night-time, heavy, light-flow, unbleached, biodegradable, mini, maxi, super-maxi, super expensive "feminine protection," it's enough to make you want to cry. Then again, it could just be PMS.

Office Grrrls

THERE'S A REVOLUTION taking place inside the government. Be warned: that neatly-dressed, well-coifed, control-top-panty-hosed clerk who answers the phone at the taxation office could be one of them.

I know what these women are capable of—I've been to one of their meetings. Thirteen of them, all government employees. They took over four rooms at a downtown hotel. Every year, this group (code name: "The Loud Crowd") infiltrates a different city. That way no one gets suspicious. I got in because of my connections. My sister is one of them.

The grand assembly Saturday night in one of the rooms was a rally to end all rallies. Fueled by pizza, vodka & oranges, and Amaretto, we talked about sex, relationships, love, marriage, kids, and farting. We sang the party rallying cries (the theme to the "Brady Bunch," "Maria," and an R-rated version of "I say potato, you say po-tah-to; you say fellatio..."). Then we went to the bar.

These women may have limited access to the upper echelons, but that doesn't mean they don't wield power. There was enough energy in this particular group to fuel the whole city. And while their panty-hose may control what nature may not, make no mistake, these women are in control of their lives.

Their demands are simple. They want love, in some cases marriage and families, but they want it on their own terms. They'll compromise, yeah, but only if their partner will too. They want good sex, but they want a good companion even more. They want someone to come home to, someone they can have fun with, who will make them laugh. Conservative demands perhaps, but honest and passionate. These women expect to be happy, it's what they were promised, and when they're not, they do something about it.

It hasn't been easy. Ranging in age from 24 to 52, these women outdid any history-book account of how far women have come in just 28 years. (And yes, they do come. They make sure of that.)

Take "Iris." She told me that when she got married in 1962 at age 20 she was "technically" still a virgin. Raised in a strict, conservative, Scottish family, "that was the way it was," she said. "When I had 'proper sex' it was awful, a real pain in the ass, not literally, of course," she laughs. Kids soon followed but not because Iris wanted them. "Convention dictated."

But eventually Iris said to hell with convention and decided to go back to work. Her husband wasn't keen on the idea—Iris's "non-job" of taking care of a house and kids had not been in *his* list of career choices. They worked it out. She insisted, he compromised. Now, at 52, Iris is the breadwinner in the family and having the time of her life. And sex is no longer a pain in the ass, unless they don't use enough lube. Iris is menopausal now and sex can sometimes give new meaning to the term "dry humping." She tried hormone treatments for a while but the K-Y generation offered her more tolerable options.

Sarah also grew up with the "marriage first, sex after" generation. She left home to marry her husband at age 19. "Sex was horrible and I thought there was something wrong with me," she says. "I didn't feel anything for this person—I was ready to charge him with rape."

Sarah left. She regrets not going to college, not having allowed herself a life between being at home and getting married. "I knew nothing about anything at the time." That first marriage turned out to be a crash course. Sarah has been happily married to her second husband for 10 years and has finally discovered her own life outside of family. As far as sex, she was part of the party consensus, these women are having the best sex of their lives.

"At 20, you're unsure of yourself, you're always trying to look good. At 40, you like yourself, you're more comfortable with yourself and with your partner, so you like sex better," Sarah admits.

With this, the room launched into a chorus of Amen, and my sister proceeded to do cartwheels across the pastel-spread of the hotel bed. (She'll never shake the high-school gymnast in her.)

At 32, Trish grew up with a much more open attitude about sex than her older colleagues. She did have sex before marriage. "Of course, I also expected to marry the first guy I did it with." She did. She had a child with him and left when she decided she didn't like how she was being treated. It hasn't been easy being single again. "People have a very different attitude towards you," she says. Not that it stops her. The singles bars were like putty in her hands that night. While every greased, Armani-suited Gino in town waited eagerly outside the no-jeans-policy-suckers-wait-outside-and-make-us-look-like-we're-the-hippest-thing-in-town club, Trish charmed us right on in, denim and all. Exactly who is in control here again?

I went home (alone) at the end of the night, inspired, in awe, and filled with the reassurances the rest of the world denies me. Women are anything but helpless and it only gets better with age.

The Loud Crowd has disbanded until next year. They've gone back to their control-tops and heels. But I know it's just a matter of time. I can see the headline now: FEMALE CIVIL SERVANTS TAKE OVER, Office Girls Unite: "Our arches have had enough and we're not gonna take it anymore."

Just Asking

MAYBE IT'S BECAUSE a 54-year-old Nancy Sinatra is making her comeback in the pages of *Playboy*, Traci Lords is on the cover of everything, and some guy named Kato is getting swarmed for autographs in shopping malls, but I suddenly feel very confused about what is going on. Now I realize that in these days of Dumb & Dumber, it's highly inappropriate to ask the really big questions, but *My Messy Bedroom* just wants to know:

1. Why is it that I can stare into my bulging closet and have absolutely nothing to wear?
2. Whatever happened to dating *before* you sleep with someone?
3. Why does his *friend* always end up liking you?
4. Why is it that you run into him unexpectedly only when you look like shit and never when you look great and are anticipating he'll show up?
5. Why is it that the ones you want to call don't and the

ones you don't, do?

6. Why do I only ever manage to pick up someone when I haven't cleaned my apartment/shaved my legs/showered or have my period/am wearing bad underwear?

7. Why *can't* he read my mind?

8. Why can't he realize that when I seem angry and get silent, it means I want to talk?

9. Why do I refuse to believe that when he seems angry and gets silent, it means he is angry and doesn't want to talk?

10. Why do I always like him less when he likes me more?

11. Why do I always like him more when he likes me less?

12. Why is it that changing-room mirrors can destroy even the best good body-image days?

13. Why can't *I* ever say, "You're right, I'm an asshole, that's just the way I am"?

14. Why are the really sweet ones so boring?

15. Why can't someone be both vulnerable *and* exciting?

16. Why don't women in movies ever have trouble achieving orgasm?

17. Why is that the more options and choices we have in life, the harder it is to get out of bed in the morning?

18. Why is it that with so many sources of information,

nobody knows anything?

19. Why are female nude dancers referred to as strippers and male nude dancers referred to as dancers?

20. Fabio?

21. Why is the person who is the opposite of everything you thought you loved about your partner suddenly the most desirable thing on Earth?

22. Why is it that when you finally build up the courage to tell him you've been cheating on him, he decides to finally tell you that he has been too?

23. Why *can't* he ever just buy you one little, itsy-bitsy surprise?

24. Why don't men ever consider that they might not exactly smell daisy fresh at all times either?

25. Why can't he ever be the one you read about who rents billboard space to declare his love for you?

26. Why is the dark mysterious stranger you meet on the train suffering from serious halitosis and insistent on "chatting" the whole way?

27. Why can't he just tell me I look great when I look great, and even once in a while when I don't?

28. Why can't I rationalize being nice to myself the way I can rationalize an unhealthy relationship?

29. Why do you care most when you shouldn't?

30. Why do fools fall in... oh, forget it.

PRINTED BY
IMPRIMERIE D'ÉDITION MARQUIS
IN JULY 1995
MONTMAGNY (QUÉBEC)